A terrific addition to a
Numbers this volume v

Alistair Begg
Senior Pastor, Parkside Church, Chagrin Fall, Ohio

Adrian has blessed us with a volume that is lively, solid and well-applied. Numbers is a neglected book and I am sure this volume will do much to reverse that. It was a great help to me in preaching through Numbers recently. Highly recommended!

Sam Allberry
local church minister, preacher and author of *Lifted* and *Connected*
Maidenhead, England

Preachers approaching the Old Testament often feel themselves to be venturing into the wilderness, perhaps nowhere more so than in the Book of Numbers. This volume provides a wonderfully concise and helpful map to orient us to the important themes of this part of the Bible, as well as stimulating suggestions to identify how it speaks to contemporary listeners. It is rooted and grounded in excellent scholarship, but connects to the needs of the ordinary preacher or Bible Study leader. Highly recommended!

Iain Duguid
Professor of Old Testament, Grove City College and Old Testament
Editor of Reformed Expository Commentary Series
Grove City, Pennsylvania

This book will be a great addition to a preacher's library; it was invaluable to me as I preached through Numbers – without it, the series would have been much poorer.

Alistair Tresidder
Local church preacher and minister, North London

The task of moving from the text of Scripture to clear and faithful exposition is challenging. This series of excellent guides aims to help the Bible teacher to observe what is there in the text, and prepare to convey its significance to contemporary hearers."

John Woodhouse
Principal, Moore College, Sydney, Australia

This teaching series, written by skilled and trustworthy students of God's Word, helps us to understand the Bible, believe it and obey it. I commend it to all Bible readers, but especially those whose task it is to teach the inspired Word of God.

Peter Jensen
Archbishop of Sydney

TEACHING NUMBERS

From text to message

ADRIAN REYNOLDS

SERIES EDITORS: DAVID JACKMAN & ADRIAN REYNOLDS

PT RESOURCES

CHRISTIAN
FOCUS

Copyright © Proclamation Trust Resources 2012

ISBN 978-1-78191-156-3

10 9 8 7 6 5 4 3 2 1

Published in 2013
by
Christian Focus Publications Ltd.,
Geanies House, Fearn, Ross-shire,
IV20 1TW, Scotland, Great Britain
with
Proclamation Trust Resources,
Willcox House, 140-148 Borough High Street,
London, SE1 1LB, England, Great Britain.
www.proctrust.org.uk

www.christianfocus.com

Cover design by DUFI-ART.com

Printed by
Bell and Bain, Glasgow

Contents

Series Preface

Apart from a few well known Sunday School stories, Numbers is almost certainly one of the most neglected books of the Old Testament. *Teaching Numbers* is, therefore, an important contribution to our series. Numbers is an important book for Christians today and Adrian's book is purposefully practical, seeking to offer real help for those involved in teaching the Bible to others. The preacher or teacher, the sermon or talk, and the listener are the key 'drivers' in this series.

The Introductory Section contains basic 'navigation' material to get you into the text of Numbers, covering aspects like structure and planning a preaching series. The 'meat' of the book then works systematically through the major sections of Numbers, suggesting preaching or teaching units, including sermon outlines and questions for Bible studies. These are not there to take the hard work out of preparation, but as a starting point to get you thinking about how to preach the material or prepare a Bible study.

Teaching Numbers brings the number of published volumes in the series to twelve. We are encouraged at how the series is developing and the positive comments from the people that really matter – those at the chalk face of Christian ministry, working hard at the Word, week in week out, to proclaim the unsearchable riches of Christ.

Our thanks must go to Celia, Adrian's wife, and Lisa Williamson for help with proof reading and checking references. As ever, our warm gratitude goes to the team at Christian Focus for their committed partnership in this project.

David Jackman & Adrian Reynolds
Series Editors
London 2013

Author's Preface

I cannot remember now why I first decided to preach through Numbers in church. It was almost certainly because I had been reading it for myself as part of my own devotions and had been struck by the importance and relevance of the message to me, and therefore for Christians today. From wherever it came, the idea soon developed and I spent a large part of 2008 preaching through Numbers at Yateley Baptist Church where I was serving as pastor.

I am particularly grateful to the members there for their long-suffering and warm appreciation of the ministry. My fellow elder and mentor, Eric Lane, helped sharpen my preaching and I would like to thank him publicly for his input. He also preached a couple of sermons in the series one of which (with his permission) I have drawn heavily upon. Two good friends, Sam Allberry and Alistair Tresidder, road-tested the material, and I am also grateful for their help and solidarity.

Subsequently, I preached the book in India in a concentrated burst and I am thankful for the feedback

9

from brothers and sisters at the Delhi Bible Institute who helped me sharpen the material further. I have also taught it as part of the Proclamation Trust's evening lectures, our Cornhill Training Course and several conferences including our Wives' Conferences and the Evangelical Ministry Assembly.

Those who have spent any time with me over the last eighteen months know that I have become rather evangelistic about this often-overlooked book of the Bible. My prayer is that this volume in our *Teaching...* series will, in the grace of God, go some way to rectifying that oversight.

Adrian Reynolds
London 2013

How to Use this Book

This book aims to help the preacher or teacher understand the central aim and purpose of the text, in order to preach or teach it to others. Unlike a commentary, therefore, it does not go into great exegetical detail. Instead it helps us to engage with the themes of Numbers, to keep the big picture in mind, and to think about how to present it to our hearers.

'Part One: Introductory Material' examines the book's themes and structure as well as seeing why it is considered a difficult book to preach. This material is crucial to our understanding of the whole book, which will shape the way we preach each section to our congregations. As a preliminary to the rest of the book, it divides the thirty-six chapters up into manageable units. This preliminary work leaves us with two major sections: 1–25 and 26–36. Each of them will form the successive parts of this book.

Parts Two and Three contain separate chapters on each preaching unit considered in Part One. The structure of each chapter is the same: it begins with a brief introduction to the unit followed by a section headed 'Listening to the text.' This section outlines the structure and context of the unit and takes the reader through a section by section analysis of the text. All good biblical preaching begins with careful, detailed listening to the text and this is true for Numbers as much as any other book.

Each chapter then continues with a section called 'From text to message.' This suggests a main theme and aim for each preaching unit (including how the unit relates to the overall theme of the book) and then some possible sermon outlines. These suggestions are nothing more than that – suggestions designed to help the preacher think about his own division of the text and the structure of the sermon. I am a great believer in every preacher constructing his own outlines, because they need to flow from our personal encounter with God in the text. Downloading other people's sermons or trying to breathe life into someone else's outlines are strategies doomed to failure. They may produce a reasonable talk, but in the long term, they are disastrous to the preacher himself since he needs to live in the word and the word to live in him, if he is to speak from the heart of God to the hearts of his congregation. However, these sections provide a few very basic ideas about how an outline on some of these passages might shape up. There are also some helpful bullet points on possible lines of application with particular focus on how lines to Christ may be drawn.

Each chapter concludes with some suggested questions for a group Bible study split into two types: questions to help *understand* the passage and questions to help *apply* the passage. Not all the questions would be needed for a study, but they give some ideas for those who are planning a study series.

The aim of good questions is always to drive the group into the text, to explore and understand its meaning more fully. This keeps the focus on Scripture and reduces speculation and the mere exchange of opinions. Remember the key issues are always, 'What does the text say?' and then 'What does it mean'? Avoid the 'What does it mean to you?' type of question. It is much better to discuss the application more generally and personally after everyone understands the intended meaning, so that the Bible really is in the driving-seat of the study, not the participants' opinions, prejudices or experiences! These studies will be especially useful in those churches where Bible study groups are able to study the book at the same time as it is preached, a practice I warmly commend. This allows small groups to drive home understanding, and especially application, in the week after the sermon has been preached, ensuring it is applied to the daily lives of the congregation.

Part 1:
Introductory Material

I

GETTING OUR BEARINGS IN NUMBERS

Introduction

The book of Numbers hardly seems promising material for a sermon series, Bible study or even a rich devotional quiet time. Not only does it seem distant from us in terms of time and geography, but the very nature of the book seems to discourage fruitful study: long lists, lots of numbers (what else?), laws, obscure stories, and, on the whole, a rather downbeat feeling of rebellion after rebellion.

But, as I hope to show, this could hardly be further from the truth: both Old and New Testament writers look back to the book of Numbers as an important part of the believers' instruction; it foreshadows Christ more clearly than perhaps any of the Pentateuch (though, of course, all of Scripture does this wonderfully); and its lessons are still relevant for a wandering generation today as we make our way towards our promised land. It ends on a high note with those we could call the heroines of the book, Zelophehad's five daughters, the women who walked by faith.

A sermon series or Bible study term in the book of Numbers should be thus fruitful and rewarding. However, it will not be without certain challenges which I will try to identify and deal with as we go. For example, there are some long and difficult passages and even our conviction about the public reading of Scripture will be challenged at this point. Numbers is one of the rare places which some English translations dare to condense (some versions do not translate 7:12-83; more of that when we get there).

As with all Scripture, the Bible-believing preacher must be in no doubt that God's Spirit has inspired material that will teach, rebuke, correct and train in righteousness. But, perhaps uniquely, the challenges of Numbers will mean that the Bible preacher or teacher will have to work hard at 'correctly handling the word of truth.'

Why is Numbers such a hard book to preach?

Perhaps a good place to start is to be honest about some of the challenges that a book like Numbers presents? Broadly these fall into five categories.

+ **The challenge of unfamiliarity.** Perhaps chief amongst our hurdles is that few people know the book of Numbers well, if at all. I did a straw poll of students here at the Cornhill Training Course and was not surprised to discover that the combined knowledge of Numbers was not really that large. Nor was mine before I began to study! And such a challenge becomes a self-fulfilling prophecy, for we tend to shy away from that which is unfamiliar, only serving to make it more so. I hope that we shall see that unfamiliarity is no cause for overlooking this rich seam of the Old Testament.

+ **The challenge of relevance.** Numbers, like many Old Testament books, seems rather distant from 21st Century life. This is compounded by the fact that most of the action takes place neither in Egypt (like Exodus) nor in Canaan (like Joshua) nor even on the brink of entry into Canaan (like Deuteronomy). Rather, we find ourselves in a nowhere place called *the wilderness*. The barrenness of such a place can easily correspond to irrelevance. However, we need to be reassured that the Bible's own commentary on Numbers (such as we find in the Psalms, in Paul and in Hebrews) sees the distance as no barrier at all; quite the opposite in fact, drawing parallels with our own spiritual journey.

+ **The challenge of genre.** For the preacher, Numbers is an enigmatic book. It contains story, law, poetry and prophecy. Perhaps no other Old Testament book contains quite this mix. Just as the preacher (and his congregation) have got into the Old Testament narrative way of thinking, then along comes a law section to break it up. No sooner have the prophet's words been ringing in our ears than we are brought to earth with a bump as we read a story about Israel's whoring. Unlike a single-genre book we need to train ourselves (and our people) to deal with variety of style and writing.

+ **The challenge of obscurity.** Talking donkeys? The ground opening up? Trial by ordeal? These are hardly everyday occurrences and the apparent obscurity of such passages makes reading, understanding and inwardly digesting all the harder; though, as we shall see, far from impossible and, ultimately, rewarding.

◆ **The challenge of violence**. As with many Old Testament books, Numbers is not afraid of violence. This comes both from the hand of the Almighty himself in wrath and judgement and in the form of battle vengeance against Israel's enemies (though the two are not unconnected). Such brutality grates on modern ears, so much so that some want to deny that the God of the Old Testament is the same as the God of the New. We believe no such thing, of course, but the preacher or teacher is duty-bound to carefully study and explain how these apparently merciless passages faithfully present our loving God.

Perhaps the best answer to all of these challenges is to ask what the book of Numbers is all about? What is its overriding theme?

The theme of Numbers: a wilderness journey

Thinking carefully about the theme that runs through the book of Numbers is an important step in the preacher's preparation. If we can determine what purpose the book serves, then we shall find understanding and preaching it a much more straightforward task. Moreover, we will have a measure against which to set all our messages to ensure they are doing what the Holy Spirit intended for the book itself.

Numbers has no key verse or passage to illuminate us. Nevertheless, even a very casual reading of the text tells us that this is a book about a journey.[1] It starts in one place and finishes in another and describes the in-between. The first sentence contains, in Hebrew, a construction which is dependent upon something that has gone before. In other words, it picks up where the previous books have left off. The last passage seems rather abrupt and leaves the reader wondering, "Well, what happens next?" This creates movement.

The setting of this journey is clear. The people of God have left Egypt (or are in the process of doing so) where they have been in slavery to Pharaoh unable to free themselves until Yahweh's[2] mighty intervention. God has called them out of this slavery, providing for their rescue and sending them on their way to the promised land. Numbers foreshadows the occupation of the land, but apart from a fleeting foray, the people never actually enter in. That is saved for the conquest book of Joshua. Numbers describes their journey to Canaan and the troubles along the way.

Dane Ortlund, director of Bible publishing at Crossway, has helpfully written out theme sentences for every Old Testament and New Testament book, relating them all to the key idea of grace which is ultimately seen in the gospel of Jesus Christ. His sentence for Numbers is worth repeating: 'Numbers shows God's grace in patiently sustaining his

---

1   Ronald Allen claims assuredly 'The theme of the book of Numbers is worship' but this seems difficult to sustain against the entirety of the book unless the word is taken in its very broadest sense. R Allan in *The Expositor's Bible Commentary Vol. 2*, Ed. FE Gaebelein and JD Douglas (Grand Rapids, USA: Zondervan, 1990), p658

2   Throughout this book I will refer to the divine name of God (represented in most Bibles using capitals: 'LORD') as Yahweh or the Lord. This is our triune God: Father, Son and Holy Spirit and it is important to our understanding of the Old Testament to see that this divine name represents him in all his fullness.

grumbling people in the wilderness and bringing them to
the border of the promised land not because of them but in
spite of them.'[3]

Iain Duguid, in his superb commentary on the book of
Numbers,[4] insightfully points out that the journey places
the book between what he calls 'salvation accomplished'
(the Exodus) and 'salvation completed' (conquest). There is
a sense in which the people have received the benefits of
the salvation Yahweh has won for them, but they have yet
to enter into all its fullness. Not surprisingly, this resonates
with every New Testament believer: 'We live between the
work of God in accomplishing our salvation at the cross
and the time when that salvation will be brought to its
consummation when Christ returns. We too live between
the times.'[5]

But how does this idea of living between the times relate
to the book of Numbers in particular? Perhaps it is worth
pausing at this point and considering the titles of the book.
Unusually, it has three.

Numbers

The name most of us will be familiar with is the name
represented in each of our English Bibles: Numbers. This
name was also in the Greek version of the Old Testament
familiar to Jesus and his followers, the Septuagint. It is
a straightforward name and entirely appropriate for a book
which has many lists and numbers. However, the primary

---

3   The full list of sentences can be accessed at http://bit.ly/9xvOQ9
(accessed 18 January 2012)

4   Iain M. Duguid, *Numbers, God's Presence in the Wilderness* (Wheaton,
USA: Crossway Books, 2006)

5   Duguid, p.19

reason for the name is the two censuses which take place in chapters 1 and 26.

Both count the number of fighting men available to Moses as he leads the people of Israel into the promised land. However, each counts a different generation. The first counts the generation who left Egypt, but their rebellion means that they fall in the wilderness. The second counts the next generation who will enter into and conquer Canaan. As we shall see, these two censuses play an important role in the book and so, far from being a title that would only appeal to accountants and actuaries, this common name is entirely appropriate as well as being illuminating.

In the wilderness

Hebrew titles often help us see the flow and trajectory of a Bible book. They are mostly found in the opening words or sentence of the text. Numbers is no different on that score, though unusually there are two Hebrew titles which are ascribed to it. The first, and most common is 'in the desert' (NIV) or 'in the wilderness' (ESV) taken from 1:1 (the third clause in Hebrew). The wilderness is the Bible's nowhere place. It is not a place in which to live or flourish, simply a place you pass through from one setting to another: 'in general, geographical regions beyond the limits of civilisation and widely perceived as disorderly and inhospitable.'[6]

Such a name conveys movement. No one wants to remain in the wilderness. However, it is not only *geographically* exact, but *spiritually* exact too. Because the people of God rebel against their Saviour they remain in this no-man's land and eventually meet their death there too. This is the

---

6   Entry in *Eerdmans Bible Dictionary* (Grand Rapids, USA: William B Eerdmans, 1987) electronic edition

title picked up by Stephen in his majestic biblical history in Acts 7 when he describes Moses as being in the 'assembly in the desert' (Acts 7:38).

It's also an appropriate name for our wanderings. Like the people of Israel the world is not our home. We have been saved but we are longing, with Abraham for the 'city with foundations, whose architect and builder is God' (Heb. 11:10). Like Stephen, a more modern hero also picks up on this language: perhaps the most famous Christian book ever written begins with John Bunyan's words, 'As I walked through the *wilderness* of this world....' (Pilgrim's Progress, my italics).

And God said…

There is another Hebrew title however. It can be variously translated 'And God said' or 'And Yahweh spoke...' It is an earlier title which fell out of use; in common with many Hebrew titles it simply picks up the first two Hebrew words of the text.[7] The phrase appears at least 45 times throughout the book. Sometimes this gives rhythm, authority and continuity to apparently disparate passages (for example, 5:1-4, 5-10, 11-31; 6:1-21, 22-27). Other times it serves as a word of grace which brings the rebellion of the people into sharp focus. God continues to speak throughout the book of Numbers, in itself a remarkable thing.

These three titles together reinforce the theme of the book which can perhaps be summarised thus: *Yahweh accompanies his people on their wilderness journey to the promised land.* The key question then becomes, "will they

---

7   Few commentaries identify this title. However it is referenced and researched by R Dennis Cole, *The New American Commentary, Numbers* (Nashville, USA: Broadman & Holman, 2000).

make it?" The Scottish preacher James Philip says their challenge is like that expressed by Shakespeare:

> There is a tide in the affairs of men,
> Which, taken at the flood, leads on to fortune;
> Omitted, all the voyage of their life
> Is bound in shallows and in miseries.
> On such a full sea are we now afloat,
> And we must take the current when it serves,
> Or lose our ventures.[8]

This is the question that Numbers answers: will the exiles take the current or lose their ventures? To answer that we need to look at the structure of the book.

Structure

Traditionally most commentators have opted for a geographical structure. Most of the action takes place in three locations: Sinai (chs. 1–12), Kadesh Barnea (chs. 13–21) and Moab (chs. 22–36). Each of the first two sections also contains a brief transitory travel section (in the first case, chapters 11 and 12, in the second, chapters 20 and 21).

This type of structure has much to commend it. First of all, it certainly conveys a progression of sorts. The action starts out at point A, travels through B and comes to an end at C. This fits with what we understood to be the journeying theme of the book. Secondly, it seems to fit neatly with chapter 33. This chapter reads like a travelogue written down by Moses at the Lord's direct command (33:2). Though many of the place names are not mentioned

---

8   Julius Caesar Act IV Scene III, quoted by James Philip, *The Preacher's Commentary, Numbers* (Nashville, USA: Thomas Nelson, 1987), p.21

elsewhere in Numbers, the three main locations are referenced in verses 15, 36 and 48.

On this basis the book splits into three and it is a popular choice with commentators. But it is not the only, nor the best choice. 'The kind of structure one sees depends on the questions one asks…[this] more traditional analysis of Numbers connects the book more closely with the Pentateuch,' argues Ashley.[9] But Ashley is only right about the geographic structure and its fit with the Pentateuch if such a structure is internally consistent within the book of Numbers itself and, therefore, with the author's original intent. I am not sure that it is. Consider the evidence:

- Whilst all three locations in the book are included in the summary chapter (Sinai in verses 15 to 16; Kadesh Barnea in verses 36 and 37; plains of Moab in verses 48 and 49) they hardly receive the emphasis one would expect if these were the three major divisions of Numbers.

- There are simply too many place names in chapter 33 that are missing from the text for it to be a summary of the book and therefore link closely with it. By my count, something like 18 of the names are unique to chapter 33.

- Although such a structure captures the idea of a journey, it ignores the narrative progression of the book. There is a downward spiral in the spiritual well-being of the people. Perhaps this can be illustrated figuratively using a graph? The journey is full of ups and downs, but on the whole the trend is downward until the latter third of the book where things improve significantly.

---

9   Timothy R. Ashley, *The Book of Numbers* (Grand Rapids, USA: William B Eerdmans, 1993), p. 2-3

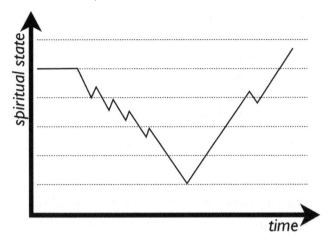

+ Plotting the action this way identifies a significant turning point in the narrative where things pick up. This is chapter 26, which happens to be the second census. A geographic outline takes no account of this division which is obvious from a careful reading of the text.

+ If the travelogue of chapter 33 is to be taken as a geographic guide, it must be noted that it nearly all focuses on the middle section. Sinai barely gets a mention and the plains of Moab, where all the action from chapter 22 onwards takes place, only gets a concluding comment (33:48-49). Once again, the descriptions simply do not fit the text if chapter 33 is to be taken as a kind of index.

There is, however, a different way to read Numbers. This has been proposed by Dennis Olson[10] and taken up by only a few commentators but, I suggest, *does* fit the text and

10   Dennis T Olson, *Interpretation, Numbers* (Louisville, USA: John Knox Press, 1996). Ronald Allan adds his own agreement: 'the direction of Olson's work is simply stunning', Allan, p. 674.

theme. According to this analysis the book of Numbers is essentially the tale of two generations. The first generation leaves Egypt, rebels and perishes in the wilderness. The second generation, born in the wilderness, believes and lives and (eventually in Joshua) gains the promised land. This structure seems to fit all the evidence:

+ It does justice to the significance of the two censuses which otherwise become simple counting exercises. On this basis, however, they mark the beginning of the story of each generation. Chapter 26 is given its rightful place as a watershed moment in the movement of the text.

+ The tone of the text is consistent with dividing at chapter 26. Prior to this point the text is rather bleak about the state of the nation. Afterwards there is much more optimism about inheriting the land.

+ This structure sits comfortably with the narrative progression of the text. We could repeat our graph, adding a few captions.

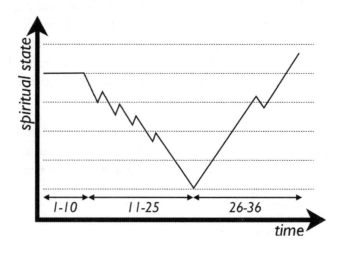

- As we shall see in just a moment, this structure is also sympathetic to the way that both Old and New Testament writers understand the meaning of the book.

- It also reflects the change in leadership which the text reinforces. Chapters 1–25 describe the era of Moses and Aaron whilst the second section carefully explains that Joshua and Eleazar are now the leaders.

- Most importantly however, this *spiritual* structure allows us to anchor our understanding of any particular passage in the general sense of the text. In the first section there is warning – an example to avoid. In the second there is encouragement, an example to emulate.

On this basis, the book has two clear sections:

- Part 1: "Death in the wilderness" *The old generation rebels and dies* (Num. 1–25)

- Part 2: "Life in the promised land" *The new generation obeys and lives* (Num. 26–36)

For sure, there are ups amongst the downs of the first section, for example the successful battle of Arad (21:1-3). There is also, possibly, a down amongst the ups of part 2 (ch. 32, though not every commentator agrees – see p. 259 for further discussion). Also, part 1 could be further subdivided as the first 10 chapters describe good times for Israel. Though they have not yet set out on their journey, they seem to be obedient and faithful. I have represented this on the graph as something of a plateau, though it must be remembered that the post-escape chapters of Exodus hardly paint this generation in a positive light.

So, perhaps we could expand the outline a little:

+ **Part 1: Death in the wilderness**
  + A good beginning (1–10)
  + An inevitable end (11–25)

+ **Part 2: Life in the promised land**
  + A new generation (26–36)

Context

It is important for us to set the biblical context for the book of Numbers. The Pentateuch tells the unfolding story of how the promises made to Abraham are being fulfilled.[11] Numbers plays an important part in this unpacking – for it focuses in particular on two of the three promises made to Abram in Genesis 12 (people, land and blessing). Whilst it is not immediately clear how the people of Numbers will be a blessing to others (at this stage they are mostly *fighting* enemies, not *blessing* them), the fulfilment of the promises regarding the number of Abram's descendants (as numerous as stars in the sky – see Genesis 15:5) and the land (Gen. 12:1) is clear.

The New Testament makes it clear that these promises are fulfilled in Christ, the seed of Abraham (see, for example, Gal. 3:16). Indeed, 'Abraham and his offspring received the promise that he would be heir of the *world*' (Rom. 4:13, my italics). The physical realities of Abrahamic fulfilment seen

---

11   'The theme of the Pentateuch is the gradual fulfilment of the promises to the patriarchs, and Numbers makes a notable contribution of the exposition of that theme. There are four elements to the patriarchal promise set out first in Genesis 12:1-3: (1) land, (2) many descendants, (3) covenant relationship with God, and (4) blessing to the nations. These four aspects of the promise all play a role in Numbers.' GJ Wenham in *The esv Study Bible* (Wheaton, USA: Crossway, 2008), p. 258.

in Numbers point towards greater and eternal spiritual realities in Christ, 'guaranteed to all Abraham's offspring… to all those who are of the faith of Abraham' (Rom. 4:16).

These are important truths to keep in mind whilst preaching or teaching through Numbers. Whilst Christians may hold different views about the ongoing nature of Israel and the place of the physical land in God's purposes, it is clear that the ultimate realities to which Numbers points are the spiritual and faith-led fulfilment of promises made to Abram and found only in Christ.

Authorship

We need only say a little about authorship. Traditionally these first five books of the Bible are known as the books of Moses, though the only clue we get that Moses is the original author of Numbers is found in 33:2. Some commentators argue that Moses cannot be the author for it is clearly self-contradictory for the most humble of men to write 'Moses was a very humble man, more humble than anyone else on the face of the earth' (12:3)! However, traditional arguments for Mosaic authorship, not least the way other Bible writers refer to these books, are still robust to give evangelicals assurance."

Doubts about authorship mean that some commentators spend inordinate amounts of time discussing whether certain portions are original or later inserts. For the purposes of Bible believing preachers and teachers such analysis is ultimately unrewarding insomuch as it casts doubt on the veracity of the text we have before us. Better, I think, to say that precise human authorship is never clarified in the text but that we are confident that the Holy Spirit 'breathed out' the book. Thus, though certain hard sections may seem out of place (conveniently for some commentators) we should always work hard to be asking "why is this here, at this place?" We shall seek to do this in the text that follows.

Rebellions

It is worth mentioning that a key feature of the central section of the book (from chapters 11 through 25) is one of rebellion. Chapter 11 opens with a very brief, general but prototypical account. The people grumble, the Lord responds in judgement, the people cry out to Moses who intercedes for them and the Lord's anger diminishes. Nearly all the rebellions that follow take the same pattern.

There are, depending on the method of counting, about 13 of these rebellions. Subsequent rebellions do not necessarily add new information all the time, other than reinforcing that the grumbling spirit of this first generation is never really changed. Even after the ultimate judgement (death in the wilderness, chapters 13 and 14) this complaining continues. Everyone is affected. Only Joshua and Caleb from the first generation ever enter the land.

Although it is difficult to convey in a sermon series or home group programme, the repetition of the rebellions itself serves a purpose. I remember watching a highly effective TV war series (*Band of Brothers*) where the bombing of the front line continued throughout the particular episode. After a while, it simply became numbing: "surely that must be the end?" I thought to myself. But it continued on. This same effective technique is being used here to make a point about the hearts of the Israelites. The fact that the rebellions keep coming and coming makes the reader feel quite numb. Though the preacher may be tempted to skip over some of these passages, to do so would be to lose the purpose of the text in painting a bleak picture of the state of a rebellious heart, unchanged by a seemingly never-ending cycle of complaint-repentance-complaint.

The table below gives some idea of these rebellions. The key one is that of the entire people (save Joshua and Caleb) against Yahweh regarding the occupation of the land (chapter 14, highlighted in the table). This is the well-known story of the spies and the primary cause of the generation dying in the wilderness.

Rebellion	Reference	Place
Assembly and hardships	11:1-3	Taberah
Assembly and the manna	11:4-34	Kibroth Hattaavah
Moses against Yahweh	11:18-21	Kibroth Hattaavah
Miriam/Aaron against Moses	12:1-2	Hazeroth
10 spies	13:31	Paran
Assembly and the conquest	14:1-4	Kadesh in Paran
Assembly and presumption	14:44	'High hill country'
Korah/Dathan/Abiram/250 leaders	16:1-3	
Assembly against Moses	16:41	
Assembly and the water	20:1-13	Kadesh in Zin
Assembly against Moses	21:4	Around Edom
Seduced by Moabites	25:1-18	Shittim
Gad & Reuben reject promised land[12]	32	Plains of Moab

---

12   See p. 259 for more information about this particular rebellion. I take the story negatively, but not every commentator agrees.

2

WHY SHOULD WE PREACH AND
TEACH NUMBERS?

Why should a 21ˢᵗ Century preacher bother with Numbers? Or, for that matter, why should a 21ˢᵗ Century *believer* bother with Numbers? There are two main reasons, both of which we get from the Bible itself.

Numbers proclaims Christ

The first is that, like all of Scripture, Numbers proclaims Christ. Our Biblical theology teaches us that, in the words of one of my daughter's Bibles, 'every story whispers his name.'[1] Jesus teaches the pair on the road to Emmaus: 'and beginning with Moses and all the Prophets, he explained to them what was said in all the Scriptures concerning himself' (Luke 24:27). 'Moses' here represents the books of Moses – the first five books of the Bible. In what way, however, does Numbers speak of Christ?

First, it speaks of him *indirectly*. The whole of the Old Testament fits together to form a unity which looks forward

---

1   Sally Lloyd-Jones, *The Jesus Storybook Bible* (Grand Rapids, USA: Zondervan, 2007)

to the coming of the Saviour of the world.[2] As such, any Old Testament passage is part of a trajectory which takes us, ultimately, to the incarnation, life, death and resurrection of Christ (and beyond, of course). In this sense we should expect to see urgent anticipation of the Messiah.

Such anticipation is sometimes seen *negatively* in terms of how desperate the state of the people is without the lasting forgiveness and life-changing power that the coming of Christ brings. Along the way in Numbers we shall find plenty of allusions and hints that make us cry out "How long, O Lord?" But it is also seen *positively*, especially in those who foreshadow Christ. Moses, in particular, is singled out in both the Old Testament and New as someone special – there is *no-one* like Moses (13:3 and Heb. 3:2-3). The various administrations of the covenant (especially the sacrifices) also look forward to Christ, the once-for-all sacrifice for sins.

There are also more **direct** proclamations of Christ. Sometimes these references are obscure without the illumination of the New Testament. Two examples will suffice:

+ The Apostle John identifies the bronze snake (Num. 21:9 – an incident which plays only a small part in the overall story) as being a foreshadowing of the lifting up of the Christ upon the cross (John 3:14-15).

+ The apostle Paul identifies the water-providing rock (Num. 20) as Christ himself, from whom the Israelites could drink both physically and spiritually (1 Cor. 10:4).

---

2   See, for example, Graeme Goldsworthy, *According to Plan* (Nottingham, UK: IVP, 1991)

When these incidents arise, the preacher must surely be faithful to the way Scripture interprets Scripture and ensure that the link to Christ is made. There is a danger, however, in seeing such indirect allusions under every rock (literally!). Some older commentaries, in particular, saw such allusions in all sorts of wonderful places. Better, I think, to make the connections where Scripture does and let the Scriptures be the best interpreter of themselves.

However, there are more direct prophecies as well. Christ is supremely Israel, God's first born and beloved son. He thus fulfils the glorious expectations that are placed upon him in Balaam's prophecies. Here is highly exalted language fit for a king: 'I see him, but not now; I behold him, but not near. A star will come out of Jacob; a sceptre will rise out of Israel' (Num. 24:17).

As with any Christian teaching, a sermon which does not proclaim Christ can hardly be described as Christian preaching, for our aim and purpose is to preach 'Jesus Christ and him crucified' (1 Cor. 2:2). I shall include in the application section of each preaching unit some ideas on how appropriate lines to Christ may be drawn.

Numbers gives us an example to avoid (or follow)

However, this does not mean that there is no exemplary role for the text. The temptation is to think that seeing Christ in the sweep of the historical context of the Old Testament precludes any ethical application. But 'we do well then to avoid setting up a false antithesis between the redemptive-historical approach and what might be called an ethical approach to the Scriptures, particularly in the historical passages. The redemptive-historical approach necessarily yields ethical application, which is an essential part of the preaching of the Word.'[3]

Both Old and New Testament writers certainly saw no embarrassment in understanding Numbers this way. It is worth a quick survey of the four key passages which comment on Numbers and the preacher might well want to preach one of the New Testament passages as an introductory sermon to the book. I have included a sample outline and a set of Bible study questions at the end of this chapter for this purpose.

Psalm 95

Psalm 95 is a brief psalm which calls God's people to sing and shout aloud to the 'Rock of our salvation.' He is the one who is a great King, the creator and sustainer of the planet, our shepherd (vv. 1-7). The application that flows from these great truths is that we should not harden our hearts towards him.

This, says the psalmist, is what happened at Meribah and Massah 'in the desert' (v. 8). These two places relate the psalm back to the account of grumbling found in Exodus 17 (Exod. 17:7). Massah means testing and Meribah means quarrelling. (Interestingly, Meribah is also the name given to a place in Numbers where a similar incident occurs – see Numbers 20:13.)

However, the psalmist seems to be thinking about the whole journey from Egypt to Canaan – not just the Exodus account – for he repeats God's condemnation, 'for forty years I was angry with that generation...' (v. 10) which itself relates not to grumbling over water but a refusal to go into the land (see Numbers 14).

---

3   Edmund P Clowney, *Preaching and Biblical Theology* (London, UK: Tyndale Press, 1962)

Therefore, the psalmist applies a broad lesson to the wandering years which is essentially this: "don't make the same mistake they did."

Hebrews 3-4

This same passage and application is picked up in Hebrews 3–4, particularly 3:7–4:13. There we have a Bible study (the Hebrews passage) on a Bible study (Ps. 95) with an extensive analysis of the psalm. The passage is far from straightforward, tackling as it does the biblical theology of rest and Sabbath. In the Old Testament 'rest' is sometimes a synonym for the promised land.

The writer argues that the warning of Psalm 95 'Do not harden your hearts' still stands today because the threat 'they shall never enter my rest' also still stands. How so? Surely when the people conquered Canaan they entered the rest? Not so, argues the writer. For then, Psalm 95 (written as it was after the conquest) could not have said 'Today.' 'Rest' must mean more than the promised land. Indeed, it means, ultimately, the Sabbath rest that God already enjoys – nothing less than eternal peace and presence with him.

That is why the promise still stands (as does the warning). This elevates Numbers and its story of being careful not to fall in the desert to the highest level. On this understanding, Numbers is a picture of our own wilderness wanderings and we must be careful to enter into our own promised land, our own 'rest' – the 'Sabbath rest for the people of God' (Heb. 4:9).

An interesting aside is that the most famous part of this Hebrews passage is set in its proper context. 'For the word of God is living and active. Sharper than any double-edged sword, it penetrates even to dividing soul and spirit, joints and marrow; it judges the thoughts and attitudes of the heart. Nothing in all creation is hidden from God's sight. Everything is uncovered and laid bare before the eyes of him to whom we must give account.' (Heb. 4:12-13). This text is often used as a comfort, but in the context of Hebrews 3 and 4 and the setting of Numbers it is actually about judgement. The word of God comes as a word of wrath in Numbers to prevent the people from entering the promised land. Hardly warming in the way we normally present it!

In fact, the whole book of Hebrews appears to be a commentary on the book of Numbers. Not only are there direct references like those above, but the book is full of allusions to Numbers material. My colleague, Dr Jonathan Griffiths[4], believes that it is not unthinkable that the writer of Hebrews had the text of Numbers "open" before him as Hebrews follows the flow so closely. At the very least, a preacher or teacher seeking to embark upon Numbers should have read through Hebrews and noted down the useful links and ideas.

Psalm 106
Psalm 106 is a long psalm beginning with the common refrain 'Praise the Lord.' It describes the history of the nation from Egypt to Ezekiel. However, the bulk of the text focuses on the events of Numbers. Verse 13 begins the Numbers story (though it does scoot back to Exodus every now and again). Many of the individual narratives warrant particular attention: the failure to listen to Joshua and Caleb (Num. 13, Ps. 106:24-27); the monumental failure at Shittim (Num. 25, Ps. 106:28-31); even Moses' failure to honour the Lord as holy (Num. 20, Ps. 106:32-33). The

---

4   Jonathan is editor of and contributor to *The Perfect Saviour, Key Themes in Hebrews* (Nottingham, UK: IVP, 2012), a collection of essays on the book of Hebrews.

events of Numbers are not recounted in the psalm in strict chronological order. Nonetheless, it is clear that something is to be gained from a review of the nation's history.

What is it? It is:

+ a call to praise the faithful Lord who brought them through it: 'Give thanks to the Lord, for he is good, his love endures forever' (v. 1) and 'Praise be to the LORD, the God of Israel, from everlasting to everlasting. Let all the people say, "Amen!" Praise the LORD.' (v. 48)

+ a plea to God to go on saving them. 'Save us, O LORD our God, and gather us from the nations, that we may give thanks to your holy name and glory in your praise.' (v. 47)

In other words, the psalmist recognises that the intrinsic nature of the people's failure in the desert remains. The people of God still need God to save them – that is their only hope.

There is a good symmetry here with the Pentateuch. Some commentators think that the five books of Psalms mirror to some extent the first five books of The Law; if this is so then this, the last psalm of Book IV, ought in some way to expound on the fourth book of the Pentateuch which just happens to be Numbers!

1 Corinthians 10:1-14
Psalm 106 is more detailed than Psalm 95 in its analysis of the wilderness wanderings and, similarly, 1 Corinthians 10 examines the accounts in more detail than Hebrews 3–4.

Again, there is clear reference to some of the post-Exodus stories. Verse 7 of 1 Corinthians 10 refers to the incident of the Golden Calf in Exodus 32. However the remaining references are almost certainly all to Numbers: verse 8 refers to Numbers 25; verse 9 refers to Numbers 21; and verse 10, though slightly obscure, probably refers to Numbers 11.

Paul is unashamed to spiritualise the journey and draw ethical lessons from it. For the physical realities had real spiritual meaning – 'they were all baptised into Moses in the cloud and the sea. They all ate the same spiritual food and drank the same spiritual drink, for they drank from the rock that accompanied them and that rock was Christ' (vv. 2-3).

This last statement is perhaps the most surprising. The rock, the miraculous source of their refreshment was itself an allusion to Christ. Paul thus makes the stories of Numbers highly relevant to Christians today, 'these things occurred as examples to keep us from setting our hearts on evil things as they did' (v. 6). So, his primary application from reading Numbers is that Christians today should not be 'idolaters' nor 'commit sexual immorality' nor 'test the Lord' nor 'grumble.'

In fact, if we think we are so secure, we'd better take care! 'Be careful that you don't fall!' (v. 12). However, for our encouragement we also learn that 'No temptation has seized you except what is common to man. And God is faithful; he will not let you be tempted beyond what you can bear. But when you are tempted, he will also provide a way out so that you can stand up under it' (v. 13) – a lesson that the wilderness generation failed to learn or apply.

We can certainly read Numbers with this ethical outlook, indeed it would be wrong not to. But how does it fit with what Clowney calls the redemptive-historical approach? 1 Corinthians perhaps provides the answer. For all along,

Christ journeyed with them. They were not alone and their ethical failure was their failure to see Christ amongst them and fix themselves upon him.

Proclaiming Christ in the Scriptures and calling people to ethical obedience to a holy God are therefore not mutually exclusive. Rather, they are gloriously one and the same thing. We could say, therefore, that Numbers gives us an example to follow as it proclaims Christ in all his glory and goodness.

The preacher or Bible group leader does not have to hold these two in tension – "a little more of Christ here, a little less ethics there." No, to see Christ in Numbers is to see both a holy God and the One who calls us to be holy and makes us holy.

I take it that we can also apply this approach *positively*. Although both 1 Corinthians and Hebrews do so *negatively* ('Don't be like them') we can infer that where Numbers is positive, we can be too. Take the daughters of Zelophehad (chs. 27 and 36). These five women walk by faith and believe in the inheritance. They are willing to do whatever is needed to claim and keep the inheritance allotted to them. They do not fall in the wilderness but, rather, are heroines of the faith. We are not to be like their father Zelophehad who did fall in the desert. But we can apply the same New Testament principle to say that we should marvel and imitate the attitude and faith of his five girls.

A possible introductory sermon: 1 Corinthians 10:1-14

It would be possible to preach an introductory sermon to Numbers from 1 Corinthians 10. The preacher must be careful doing this of course, because the temptation will be to rip the Corinthian text out of its context in the epistle in which it is found. Further work is required to think carefully how this can be done faithfully.

Nevertheless, 1 Corinthians 10 is an important New Testament control on how to read the Old Testament book of Numbers. An introduction could focus on the idea of learning lessons from the past, perhaps with the well-known quote: 'History doesn't repeat itself, but it does rhyme' (attributed to Mark Twain, though there is no record of him ever saying it!). In other words, it is always wise to learn from the past; indeed the Apostle Paul is certain that we must do so.

He draws parallels between the people of Numbers and the Corinthians to whom he writes. His references to 'eating' and 'drinking' (v. 3) are almost certainly a reference to the Lord's Supper – the subject of this section of the epistle. But the point is clear – there is a connection between the historical people and God's people today. 'These things occurred as examples to us to keep us from setting our hearts on evil things as they did' (v. 6). The lessons are clear and delineated in the text:

+ Do not be idolaters (v. 7)

+ Do not commit sexual immorality (v. 8)

+ Do not test the Lord (v. 9)

+ Do not grumble (v. 10)

Each of these headings could be referred back to the relevant section in Numbers (or, for point 1, to Exodus). The conclusion to the passage is very encouraging and sets the tone for reading Numbers positively. Verses 11-14 contain both warning ('be careful that you don't fall!') and exhortation. We need not make the same mistakes that the wanderers did. When we are tempted 'he will also provide a way out so that you can stand up under it' (v. 13). 'Therefore, my dear friends, flee from idolatry' (v. 14).

It is helpful to point out that the wilderness people had this same promise for the rock that accompanied them was Christ (v. 4). So, in reading Numbers, we must never say that they were different from us and so failure was inevitable. No! They had Christ with them, just as we do today.

A possible introductory Bible study on 1 Corinthians 10:1-14

This Bible study introduces the themes of Numbers by considering one of the key commentaries on the book: Paul's comments in 1 Corinthians 10:1-14.

Questions to help understand the passage

1. What is the context of this warning to the Corinthians? See 1 Cor. 8 and 1 Cor. 10:14-22.

2. What links or similarities are there between the people who wandered in the desert and the Corinthian Christians (vv. 1-5)?

3. What surprises you about what Paul says? How does that help us understand Numbers better?

4. What is the main lesson to be learnt (v. 6)?

5. What four sub lessons does this break down into (vv. 7-10)?

6. Try to see if you can link these lessons to specific incidents in Exodus or Numbers. Use a cross-reference Bible to help you.

7. What warnings are contained in verses 12-14?

8. What encouragements are contained in verses 12-14?

Questions to help apply the passage

1. How does this passage help us read the stories in Numbers?

2. The examples Paul quotes all seem quite extreme. How can we apply them to our lives?

3. How does having Christ with us on our journey make a difference to how we live?

4. What does verse 13 mean in practice? How can we use it positively to avoid the mistakes of the wilderness generation?

3

IDEAS FOR PREACHING OR TEACHING
A SERIES ON NUMBERS

Numbers is a long book – 36 chapters made up of a mix of dense (and sometimes action-packed) narrative, long law sections, very long lists of names and numbers and a fair sprinkling of prophecy. There are also some very familiar texts, whether it is the messianic prophecy of 24:17 or phrases that have passed into proverbial use, such as 'be sure your sin will find you out' (32:23).

It seems a rather daunting task for the preacher or person tasked with planning the Bible study series. Where to start? Here are some initial observations about a series on Numbers:

- A series on Numbers should seek to be faithful to the movement and progression of the text because these are critical to the overall theme of the book. Therefore, any series needs to capture the incessant and deteriorating nature of Israel's rebellion. For example, it is unlikely to present the book fairly if the preacher simply selects

one rebellion passage on the basis that "one is enough."
He will not capture the progression.

+ A series on Numbers should not seek to avoid either
  difficult or apparently 'boring' sections. These are part
  of the text, divinely inspired. Thus, they play a role.
  Charles Simeon's discourses only start at chapter 5,
  chapters 1 to 4 presumably holding little appeal. This
  is surely an oversight. [1]

+ Realistically there will need to be some condensing to
  make this into a manageable series. This book is based
  on a 17 part series which I think is the minimum
  needed to preach the book reasonably thoroughly.
  Even so this condenses many of the sections which
  could easily be preached more slowly. In the notes
  I suggest alternative ways of breaking these sections
  into shorter ones, making for a longer series.

+ I have also suggested a briefer outline. This will
  introduce the book, perhaps whetting people's
  appetites, but is unlikely to be thorough enough to
  do justice to the themes and progression mentioned
  above. Such a series may be useful to introduce the
  book before a longer series in small groups.

I should mention here that I don't generally publish sermon
titles in advance of a message. If you are one of those
preachers who likes creative and interest-stirring titles then
my titles below may seem rather dull and lifeless. Over to
you!

---

1   Charles Simeon, *Horae Homileticae Volume 2* (London, UK: Samuel
Holdsworth, 1836)

Here is an outline based on dividing Numbers up into 17 sections:

1. Numbers   (1–4)

2. Purity   (5–6)

3. Worship   (7–8)

4. Preparation   (9–10)

5. Discontent   (11–12)

6. Rebellion   (13–14)

7. Grace   (15)

8. Rejection   (16–18)

9. Cleansing   (19)

10. Salvation   (20–21)

11. Blessing   (22–24)

12. Seduction   (25)

13. Beginnings   (26–30)

14. Victory   (31)

15. Disunity   (32)

16. Anticipation (33–35)

17. Inheritance (27 & 36)

This is the outline we will use in this book. A shorter series which introduces Numbers might pick up on several of these chapters (but probably not longer sections). For example, over six weeks, one could preach:

1.	Numbers	(1–4)	introducing the book and the theme
2.	Rebellion	(13–14)	outlining the key rebellion
3.	Salvation	(20–21)	demonstrating God's grace
4.	Blessing	(22–24)	showing God's blessing and promise
5.	Victory	(31)	explaining God's ideal battle plan
6.	Inheritance	(27 & 36)	focusing on the promised land

As stated above, the trouble with such an outline is that it will be much harder for the preacher to stay faithful to the overall tone and tenor of the book. The preacher who wants to preach a shorter introductory series can still use this book to help preach the selected units shown in the shorter list above.

Preaching Old Testament narrative

This is not the place for a detailed study of how we should faithfully preach or teach Old Testament narrative. However, it is worth observing that the bulk of the Numbers material falls into this tricky category. Though Numbers also includes prophecy, poetry and law, the preacher will find that most of his time is occupied with narrative.

When seeking to understand a narrative, it is often best to divide it up into acts and scenes, much like a stage play. Although I have not always used this terminology, that is what I have sought to do in this book. Each section begins with a review of the text trying to understand the flow of the story. A preacher who is trying to be true to the text will not want to lose this flow or the colour that narrative often contains. It is all too easy to divide a passage up along propositional lines and rob the story of any pace and dynamism.

However, the preacher is doing more than simply retelling the story. He is trying to draw out gospel principles which can be applied to hearers' hearts. The sample sermon outlines included in this book attempt to highlight those principles in action. They would not necessarily form the exact outline for a sermon: some preachers, for example, prefer descriptive headings for sermons; others prefer applicatory headings. There are no hard and fast rules. But whichever approach is taken the preacher needs to be communicating the principles in the context of the text in which they were written; they cannot be detached from the Numbers story or else the preacher can hardly be said to be preaching Numbers.[2]

Particular challenges in teaching Numbers

Numbers presents some particular challenges for the preacher. Not least amongst these is the challenge always present in the Old Testament of preaching Christ. As the book progresses I will try to explain how best this can be done in this particular book. There are also one or two particular issues peculiar to this one book.

Were the first generation true believers?

Time and time again we see the wrath of God against his rebellious people resulting in judgement and death. Ultimately this means that none of the first generation are

---

2   This whole question is addressed much more comprehensively in Steven D. Mathewson, *The art of preaching Old Testament narrative* (Grand Rapids, USA: Baker Academic, 2002)

allowed to inherit the promised land, they all fall in the wilderness. As we have already seen, the New Testament writers see this as a sober warning to Christians to keep going and 'make every effort to enter that rest' (Heb. 4:11).

One question that readers regularly ask is what this says about the spiritual state of those who fell in the desert. Were they saved? Are they true heart-believers? And what does that mean for Christians who appear to fall away? The latter question is perhaps best left for the commentators on Hebrews, but the first requires an answer.

Unsurprisingly, it's a question that the text of Numbers never seeks to answer. We can certainly say that there are some who will *not* inherit the land but who *are* true believers. Chief amongst these is Moses himself. We can say with certainty that Moses is now with the Christ he prefigured (see, for example, the account of the Transfiguration in Mark 9). Yet his 'rash words' (Ps. 106:33) prevent him from entering into the inheritance.

We must therefore suppose that amongst the first generation who died in the wilderness (603,550 men plus women too), there were true believers – those who had circumcised their hearts. However, although Numbers speaks about individuals, it also deals with the nation as a whole. It is clear, for example, in Numbers 14:1-4 that the corporate nation is at fault, not just individuals within it.

And this is how the commentary passages like Psalm 106 or Hebrews 3–4 analyse the text. The Bible writers don't tend to pick out individuals and say "don't do what he/she did." They focus on the nation and say to believers today, "don't make the same mistakes." The Bible preacher or teacher must be true to this kind of instruction and not attempt to impose questions and answers onto the text that the text never seeks to ask or answer.

Preaching long passages

A more practical question is one of length. I've timed myself reading aloud through Numbers 1–4. It took fifteen minutes, reading at a rather fast rate. If, as I propose, Numbers 1–4 might be one section to be preached in a sermon series on the book, how will such a reading be incorporated into a service? Fifteen minutes (or more, probably) seems a long reading, by any measure!

Numbers 1–4 is one of the longest units I have proposed but does that mean that it is impractical to preach it? By no means! Perhaps our default position should be that the entire passage to be preached should be read – and that is certainly more manageable in a Bible study. However, it would be possible for a preacher to give a guided reading of a passage summarising sections of it or drawing attention to certain parts as he goes.

This was often the practice of some of the Victorian preachers such as Charles Spurgeon or Archibald Brown[3] and it served very well. It would also allow comment on some of the more difficult aspects of the text (for example the so-called "trial-by-ordeal" of Numbers 5:11-31) which would then mean that the preacher could preach the passage rather than using all his allotted time making an apologetic for some difficult ideas.

Alternatives are to encourage a congregation to read a passage beforehand (this will work better with some congregations than others) or to sometimes read longer passages, sometimes not – ensuring that the congregation appreciate in general the importance of public reading.

---

3   Brown's reading method is explained in Iain M. Murray, *Archibald G. Brown, Spurgeon's Successor* (Edinburgh, UK: Banner of Truth Trust, 2011).

Don't be afraid of lists. They are inspired too and often the way that they are written makes a point in itself. For example the repetition of Numbers 7 makes a very strong point about the unity of the tribes which is lost if the rhythm and cadence of the repetition is missing.

One further idea we use in our church is that we combine the sermon series with a home group series and the home groups discuss the morning sermon with a particular view to application and praying in lessons. Other churches I know study the passage the week before it is preached. In such a set up the preacher can read a shorter portion and then ask the small group leaders to make sure the full passage is read, giving the best of both worlds.

Part 2
Death in the Wilderness
(Numbers 1–25)

I
Numbers (1–4)

Introduction

Numbers 1 begins with a military counting exercise. Its purpose is to identify all those men who are able to fight to enter the promised land, Canaan (v. 3). They have left Egypt under the sovereign hand of God who has himself destroyed their chief enemy as the waters of the Red Sea covered them over. This is the immediate context of the entirety of the book, introduced by that important phrase 'after the Israelites came out of Egypt' (v. 1).

This is the 'first day of the second month of the second year'[1] – i.e. thirteen months on from the Exodus. But the people are still at the foot of the mountain, the journey has not yet begun. It's important to note that it's not a long journey. At this stage any idea of a forty year wandering is simply not in view. In fact the people reach the brink of the promised land fairly quickly (and certainly by chapter 13).

---

1   Numbers is not strictly chronological. For example, the dedication of the tabernacle (ch. 7) takes us back to Exodus 40, one month earlier than 1:1.

As has been noted in the introduction, the text begins with a Hebrew construction that usually has a preceding dependent clause – there is right from the start a sense of movement and progression – as though champion sprinters or runners are waiting on their blocks ready to go.

An initial reading seems to suggest little more than administrative niceties in the count. However, a closer look will reveal a rich seam of material for the preacher or teacher. It is important to see a common refrain running through this introductory material which follows the formula 'he did all that the Lord commanded' (see 1:19, 54; 2:34; 3:16, 42, 51; 4:37, 41, 45, 49). Once the journeying begins, it soon disappears.

The total for this military count (603,550) is identical to the tabernacle count in Exodus 38:26. The sanctuary shekel collection was almost certainly based on this military account explained in more detail here in Numbers (i.e. the actual counting was only done once). More importantly, this beginning echoes the beginning of the book of Exodus which starts with a count of those who went *into* Egypt (70). The number who left was significantly larger!

Listening to the text

Context and structure

Essentially the section breaks down into two:

+ The *military* census
  + Instructions for the military census (1:1-19)
  + Results from the military census (1:20-46)
  + Explanation of the omission of Levi from the census (1:47-54)
  + Camping and marching orders (2:1-34)

+ The *spiritual* census
  + Presentation of the tribe of Levi to Aaron to be his helpers (3:1-13)
  + Results from the spiritual census together with responsibilities (3:14-39)
  + The redemption of the first born by the Levites (3:40-51)
  + Detailed description of the work of the clans (4:1-33)
  + Summary of spiritual census (4:34-49)

Working through the text

Instructions for the military census (1:1-19)

The standard introductory formula ('The Lord spoke') begins the set of instructions for Moses. They are not complicated – he is to count every male over twenty, breaking the totals down by clan (tribe) and family (tribal sub-unit). Aaron is to help him and he can appoint family heads from each tribe to assist. The names of the helpers are set out, one from each tribe, though none from Levi (who are not counted yet) and two from the half tribes of Joseph, Ephraim and Manasseh (who for the purposes of Numbers will always be considered as two separate tribes). Moses and Aaron obey absolutely. There is even no delay in the count beginning (compare 1:1 and 1:18). It all seems to have worked very smoothly indeed.

Results from the military census (1:20-46)

The next section lists the results using a standard formula. Each tribe is different. The largest is Judah (74,600) and the smallest is unsurprisingly one of the half tribes (Manasseh with 32,200). The variation in numbers have a ring of truth about them – a fabricated account would have been much more mono-numeric. Moreover, significant variations are easily explained mathematically by small differences in early generations.

The total number of males over twenty comes to 603,550 (1:46). If we assume a similar number of females and then the same number of children, this implies a total exodus of well over 2 million.

These large numbers are not without their problems. Sceptical historians point out that growth from 70 to over two million in 430 years is possible but unlikely. Moreover, they estimate that the population of Egypt was around three million at the time so a slave population of something approaching that seems improbable. The logistics of movement and food, they say, are just too difficult for such a number.

These objections can satisfactorily be answered (improbable is not the same as impossible). More problematic is the link between this census and the spiritual census. According to 3:40-43, the Levites were to be taken as substitution for the first born of each family totalling 22,273. If the 603,550 males are distributed across 22,273 families then we must infer that 'the average mother must then have had more than 50 children.'[2]

Various solutions have been suggested. Chief of these is that we have misunderstood the Hebrew word *elep*, rendered 'thousand'. For example, the exact wording of verse 53 reads 'nine and fifty thousand [*elep*] and three hundred.' Several commentators have suggested alternative readings for the word, perhaps meaning 'military unit.'

Although an important question in understanding the exact nature of the text, this question does not need to be

2   Gordon J. Wenham, *Tyndale Old Testament Commentary, Numbers* (Nottingham, UK: IVP, 1981), p. 70

the main feature in a sermon or Bible study. Perhaps we are best to agree with Ashley: 'in short we lack the materials in the text to solve the problem. When all is said and done we must admit the answer is elusive.' However we read the text we see, he argues, 'symbols of relative power, triumph, importance and the like.'[3] When preaching this passage I was content to let the numbers stand as they are presented in the text. The teaching point (see below) is clear. Technical commentaries contain more detailed discussion of the issues surrounding the large numbers.

Explanation of the omission of Levi from the census (1:47-54)
The tribe of Levi is not counted in the military census and 1:47-54 explains why. They are to serve in the tabernacle, not as priests, but as carriers, caretakers and guards. Anyone else who approaches the tabernacle will die (1:51). They thus fulfil a function of preserving the people from inappropriately approaching the presence of Yahweh. Their precise tasks will be explained in chapters 3 and 4.

Camping and marching orders (2:1-34)
Chapter 2 repeats some of the census results but in the context of how the camp is to be set up. Each of the twelve tribes is assigned to a three-tribe unit, a division (headed up by Judah, Reuben, Ephraim and Dan). These are not just camping instructions, but marching instructions too: 'they will set out in the same order as they encamp' (2:17).

The position of the Levite clans will be explained in chapter 3. The tabernacle is at the heart of both the camping arrangements and the marching order. Taken together, the camp plan looks something like this:

---

3   Timothy R. Ashley, *The Book of Numbers* (Grand Rapids, USA: William B Eerdmans, 1993), p. 66

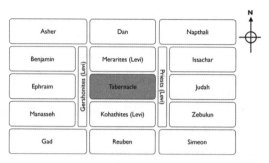

Presentation of tribe of Levi to Aaron to be his helpers (3:1-13)
Verses 1 to 4 of chapter 3 re-introduce (from Leviticus)
the family tree of Aaron. Aaron had four sons: Nadab,
Abihu, Eleazar and Ithamar. The first two are already dead
(v. 4, see also Leviticus 10). Eleazar and Ithamar (and later
Eleazar's son Phineas) will serve as priests for the duration
of Numbers. At this point in time only these amongst the
Levites are counted as priests. The vast majority of the tribe
have physical and administrative duties.

In fact, they are to guard the tabernacle. The NIV softens
the text with phrases such as 'assist', 'perform duties' and 'take
care of' (vv. 6-8) but these all translate one Hebrew phrase
meaning 'guard' (ESV). This important task (already outlined
in chapter 1) is both one for the camp and one for the road.
The Israelites hardly need protection from the furnishings
(v. 8) when they are hidden away inside the Tabernacle. Once
on a cart, however, the Levites' role is necessary.

Verses 11-13 outline the substitutionary nature of the
Levites' role which will be further expanded in chapter 4.

*Results from the spiritual census together with responsibilities
(3:14-39)*
The Levites are to be counted too, just not in the military
census. As the count is reported we also discover the roles
the clans (sub-units of the tribe) will play. The Gershonites

camp to the west and guard the soft furnishings (coverings, hangings and so on). The Kohathites camp to the south and guard the furniture of the Tabernacle (the ark, the altars, the table and so on). The Merarites camp to the north. They guard the various pegs, ropes and stakes that are required to keep the soft furnishings in place. Moses and Aaron are Kohathites, from the clan of Amram (Num. 3:19).

The redemption of the first born by the Levites (3:40-51)
Previously we saw how the Levites were given to Aaron to help guard the Tabernacle. Now we discover more details about the unique arrangement this tribe has. The firstborn sons of Israel became the possession of Yahweh at the time of the tenth plague (see Exodus 13:2, 22:29-30 and 34:19-20). Now it becomes clear that the Levites will substitute for the first born, taking their place. The same rule will apply to the first born cattle and the cattle of the Levites (v. 41).

There is a complication however. What if the number of first born males in Israel and the number of Levites do not match? The section beginning at verse 44 provides for this eventuality. Any excess first born males over and above the number of Levites can be bought back for 5 shekels each. There were actually 273 such cases (v. 46). This money is called redemption money and belongs to Aaron (v. 51).

As elsewhere in the Old Testament, particularly in the Law, there is a strong theme of substitution and redemption here and though the preacher should avoid directly linking it to Christ (there does not seem to be any biblical warrant to do so), it is hard not to see some of the key ideas that will define the atonement taking shape.

We have already thought about the problems with large numbers. One further possibility is that the arrangement of this section applied to only first born males *since the Exodus*. In other words, the Passover achieved the redemption of the first born and this new provision is to account for the first born children in the 13 months that have elapsed. On this basis, the 22,273 males are not the number of families in Israel, but the number of *new* families since the Exodus. In a population upwards of 2 million this is not an improbable number.

Detailed description of the work of the clans (4:1-33)
Chapter 4 describes the work of the clans in more detail. The order is now changed and the clans are described in order of importance of the work (they were previously described in birth order). Four types of work are described using different Hebrew words and phrases translated variously as 'serve', 'come on duty' and 'work'. The Hebrew terms more accurately represent the variety of the work they are given: *guard duty* (4:27, 28, 31, 32), *skilled labour* (4:3), *manual labour* (4:3, 19, 23, 24, 26, 27) and *ministry* (4:12-14).

Verses 5-15 operate as a kind of packing list for Aaron rather than a carrying list for the Kohathites because by the time the Kohathites get involved they will not be able to see which item is which. The Kohathites are probably given this most important of tasks because theirs is the clan of Moses, Aaron and Miriam. The hides of sea-cows (throughout this passage, NIV) is better translated goat-skins (ESV).

There is an apparent inconsistency here with regard to age ranges. Previously, the Levites have not been set an age range (ch. 3). Here the limit is 30-50 (see vv. 3, 23, 30). In 8:24 the limit becomes 25-50. The first difference is easily explained. Doing guard duty does not require age restriction. The work of chapter 4, however, is mostly physical and so age limits are applied. Numbers 8:23-26 makes it clear that the older men (past 50) are not required for carrying duties but are still to report for 'duties [guard duty] at the Tent of Meeting' (8:25-26).

Rabbinic interpretation assumed a five year apprenticeship to account for the difference in starting age between the two passages. However, there is no evidence for this. The carrying can only be done by a finite number of men, so it is possible that by chapter 8 it was realised that more men were required than first thought, hence the lowering of the beginning age to 25. We can't really be absolutely certain.

Summary of spiritual census (4:34-49)
The totals of those coming to work are now summarised. There are 2,750 Kohathites, 2,630 Gershonites and 3,200 Merarites. This 30-50 years-old total (8,580) is significantly lower than the total Levites aged a month or more (22,000 from 3:39) shedding some light on the distribution of ages in the Levite clan.

From text to message
There is a great deal of material here and the preacher or teacher will need to decide how much of it to use in a sermon or study. I have suggested an approach taking the whole of the four chapters as one unit given that they are all about counting the people. Nevertheless, there are two distinct counts for two distinct purposes (fighting and serving) and the preacher may want to take these one by one. However, they make some of the same points, so I chose to take them together.

Getting the message clear: the theme
Yahweh has faithfully rescued and grown the people of Israel, just as he promised to Abraham. This numerous nation can now journey to and conquer the promised land, God's presence going with them.

Getting the message clear: the aim
We need to rejoice in the faithfulness of God and fix our eyes upon our Saviour Christ Jesus as we journey to our promised land.

A way in
It is important to tackle up front the ennui that some Christians find in numbers, lists, genealogies and the like. There are plenty of these in Numbers and elsewhere in the Scriptures. Thus, seeing them as inspired and helpful *here* will set listeners up for a lifetime of reading the Bible. Here is one way it could be done.

Lists of numbers and names seem pretty unexciting, boring even. But consider that a cricket fan can spend hours analysing the batting averages. Parents spend hours poring over school league tables which to most people are incredibly dull. Prospective patients (or their families) look up local hospital facts and figures while waiting for surgery. Statistics become interesting when you're interested in the stories and facts behind them. So it is with these early chapters of Numbers. See the facts behind the numbers and suddenly these lists will come alive and help us journey with Christ our Rock to our promised land.

Ideas for application

+ The faithfulness of God to his covenant promises is, and continues to be, the root of our relationship with him.

+ God has rescued us from slavery and in Christ we are the true heirs of Abraham.

+ The presence of God in the tabernacle is a reminder that God is 'Immanuel', God with us. Jesus himself 'tabernacled' amongst us (John 1:14). Paul is careful to note that Christ the Rock travelled with the people of Israel.

+ The travel plans are arranged to ensure that not only is the Lord at the heart of camping, marching and (we assume) fighting, but that everyone is focused towards his presence.

+ The nature of the census is a reminder that God's people are an army called to fight, and to fight *together*.

+ The journey itself is a reminder that there is a temporal gap between the salvation event and the full enjoyment of all its benefits.

Suggestions for preaching

Sermon 1

A sermon on the whole section needs to pick up on the underlying themes. The beginning needs to introduce the idea of a journey from the place of slavery (Egypt) to the promised land (Canaan). The question Numbers asks and answers is, will they make it? And how? What do they need to know as they journey?

+ **The Lord is gracious in his salvation.** This first point could set the context for the whole book which is that salvation has happened: 'after the Israelites came out of Egypt' (1:1). However, they must not think that, having been saved, everything is done. There is an inheritance to lay hold of. Salvation has begun and must be completed.

+ **The Lord is faithful in his promises.** It is impossible not to see parallels with the number who went *into*

Egypt (70), nor to fail to be amazed at how the nation has grown, despite the efforts of Pharaoh. Now here are 603,550 fighting men leaving 430 years later. God has done what he promised on oath to Abraham. The people are now as numerous as grains of sand on the seashore or the number of stars in the sky (Gen. 15). Moreover, he promised they would exit Egypt in abundance (Gen. 15.14).

This faithfulness is *the* key truth that the travellers need to know because the same promise contains the words 'the whole land of Canaan…I will give as an everlasting possession to you and your descendants' (Gen. 17.8).

+ **The Lord is powerful in his presence.** This journey is not to be a stroll in the park. Why else would there be a military count? The people are going to have to fight! And it will be more than a battle; it will need to be a campaign, because the land is inhabited by various tribes and peoples. How will they succeed? Because they have the Lord as the power in their midst. The camping and marching order is so designed that the Tabernacle, the place of God's presence is at the centre. A whole tribe is set apart to maintain safely this presence in the midst of the people. They will succeed as they fight in the power of the Almighty.

These are lessons that are directly applicable to New Testament believers as they journey from salvation achieved to salvation completed. Our only hope is the salvation God has already given us in Christ, the faithfulness of the Father's promises and the mighty presence of the Holy Spirit.

Sermon 2

A different sermon might focus more narrowly on the military census. The preacher would still want to make the points above. However, in addition, he would want to bring out some of the detail that the passage presents. For example, there is a unity about this count that will be important for Numbers. Though from different tribes, the people must fight together (this theme will re-occur on several occasions). More can be made of the tribal arrangement (perhaps with a plan) showing just how central the Tent of Meeting is. Moreover, there is necessarily clear order and structure which is not to be despised but makes fighting and journeying more straightforward. Some, though, are set apart to make sure that the relationship with their mighty God is maintained; in other words, they do not fight and travel apart from walking closely with Yahweh.

Sermon 3

Even more focused would be a message based on the camp arrangement (chapter 2). Points could include:

+ The camp is centred on Yahweh and his presence. Everyone is turned towards it and though access is restricted, everyone has the right focus.

+ Everyone has a part to play, the very design of the camp is intended to be inclusive.

+ Yahweh, however, is not accessible. His holiness precludes the people from enjoying intimate, personal contact with him which they both need and can't have. Even Moses and Aaron are camped *outside* the Tabernacle.

Sermon 4

Moving more slowly through the text would necessitate a sermon based on the Levites (chapters 3 and 4). The strong theme of redemption and substitution would need to be brought out as would the primary role of guarding the Tabernacle, ensuring that Israelites do not approach the presence of Yawheh, for that would be fatal. How we long for access to his direct presence!

Suggestions for teaching

Questions to help understand the passage

1. How many people went into Egypt (see Exodus 1:5)? Using the passage, make an estimate of how many left (1:46 and 3:39).

2. Now read through God's promises to Abraham in Genesis 17:3-8. How does the Numbers data back up what God says to Abraham?

3. What kind of census is described in chapter 1? What does that tell us about what the Israelites should expect?

4. Why are the Levites not counted in this census (1:47-54)?

5. What is at the centre of the camping/marching plan in chapter 2? Why is that?

6. What kind of work will the Levites do? It is outlined in chapter 3 and then explained in more detail in chapter 4. Try to work out what each of the three clans are to do.

7. Why are these roles so important?

8. What other important function with respect to Yahweh do the Levites fulfil (see 3:40-51)?

Questions to help apply the passage

1. What sort of journey are Christians on? Where have we come from? Where are we going?

2. God made his presence known in the Tabernacle. How does God accompany our journey today?

3. How does reading about the Israelites' journey help us in ours?

4. Why do we get embarrassed about using military language to describe the church today? What does the New Testament say about fighting? (See, for example, Ephesians 6).

5. What clues are there in the passage that God cannot be approached by anyone? How has the work of Christ changed this?

6. What is the refrain that occurs throughout the passage? (See 1:19, 54; 2:34; 3:16, 42, 51; 4:37, 41, 45, 49.) What should our response be to the presence of Christ on our journey?

2
PURITY (5–6)

Introduction

Four apparently unconnected sets of laws follow immediately after the census arrangements. However, on closer inspection we see that the four stories are closely connected in two ways. First, they are all concerned with purity:

+ the first story (5:1-4) tackles purity in the camp;

+ the second (5:5-10) deals with purity in relationships;

+ the so-called "trial by ordeal" (5:11-31) addresses purity in marriage;

+ finally, the rules for Nazirites (6:1-21) are concerned with purity in service.

The sections are also joined together by the common introductory phrase (and one of the Jewish titles of Numbers) 'The Lord said...'

Taken together, these regulations affirm the importance of purity amongst God's people: God himself is present in the camp (5:3) and his journeying people must live accordingly. The priestly blessing that closes this section (6:22-27) is best seen as connected to the purity that the people of God display. The Old Covenant promises of blessing are conditional on the response of Yahweh's people (see, for example, Deuteronomy 28:1).

Listening to the text

Context and structure

The text divides neatly up into the four sections outlined above. Each presents its own challenges, though it is the trial by ordeal which seems, at first glance, most problematic for modern readers and for the preacher.

The section follows on from the census and camping arrangements of chapters 1–4. Those chapters are the foundational principles that need to be established if the people of God are to march to war and conquer the promised land. However, we need to be clear that entering and enjoying the land is not simply a matter of fighting for God. It matters to God how we journey and the end will not always justify the means (as the stories of Numbers will make abundantly clear); hence the focus on purity.

Each of the sections follows a familiar pattern, namely instruction from the Lord followed by details of the precise requirements. The first section also ends with a common refrain in this first part of Numbers: 'They did just as the Lord commanded Moses.' At present the people are obedient and faithful. The downward regression has not yet begun.

Working through the text

Purity in the camp (5:1-4)

The first section deals with purity in the camp. Those who are unclean because of infection or discharge or contact with dead bodies are to go outside of the camp precincts; no one is exempt. Some commentators identify this as a practical law, like an early health and safety guideline, but the text is more profound. Such a motivation might well apply to an infectious person; however, in the case of contact with the dead body, a hygiene ruling would place the *dead body* outside the camp, not the person who had contact with it. The issue is deeper than a healthy lifestyle.

All becomes clear in verse 3. The camp is the place where the Lord dwells. Certainly, his particular presence is in the Tabernacle, the Tent of Meeting. But the tabernacle cannot possible contain him and he is present with his people (see Deuteronomy 4:7). This short section concludes with the standard obedience formula.

Purity in relationships (5:5-10)

Verses 5-10 deal with the need for purity in relationships and what must happen when things go wrong. Sin is not isolated from our relationship with God. A realistic view of sin is that when a man or woman 'wrongs another in any way' they are 'unfaithful to the Lord.' The actual phrase is 'breaks faith with' and is repeated in the next section in verse 12. King David has a similar view of the nature of sin, expressed in Psalm 51:3-4.

When such an individual 'realises his guilt' (ESV, v. 6) he must take a number of steps. First, he must confess his sin (v. 7). Then he must make 'restitution for his wrong' which means making good and adding a proportion (one fifth).

Verse 8 deals with the very practical situation where no living relative is available to receive the restitution. In this case recompense goes to the priest. This last circumstance is not considered in the equivalent Levitical rules. However, it would not have been long before the situation arose, so the regulations of Numbers 5 cover the eventuality.

This is not the entire story, however. The confession and restitution must be accompanied by a sin offering, a 'ram with which atonement is made for him.' This offering is the guilt offering of Leviticus 7.1-7. Both in language and offering, we see clearly that sin has both a horizontal and vertical effect. Verses 9 and 10 seem slightly obscure, but are simply reinforcing the fact that a contrite man has no claim on the offering he brings to the priest. He cannot, for example, claim some of it back as his own.

Purity in marriage (5:11-31)
The remainder of chapter 5 deals with a particular instance of breaking faith: suspected adultery. We must be honest about such passages and say that for some hearers they will sound medieval or unjust. The so-called "trial by ordeal" perplexes many modern readers reminding them of the witch-ducking trials of the Middle Ages. In these ordeals an accused woman was tied to a stool and lowered under water for some minutes. If she managed to survive the ordeal, she was obviously a witch and was burned. If she died from the ordeal, she was declared innocent – not much fairness or justice there.

Such ordeals were not unknown in the ancient world. Accounts contemporary to Numbers tell, for example, of a trial by ordeal for adultery which involved a woman placing her hand in boiling water. The guilty woman was unharmed (but subsequently punished); the innocent woman suffered burns but was declared free.

The barbarity and unfairness of these trials can make us very defensive when we read accounts like this one in Numbers. However, it is important to see that this trial is quite different from those outlined above. Firstly, this trial is completely safe for the innocent woman. There is no harm that comes from drinking the bitter water (5:27-28). It may have a nasty taste, but nothing worse. Yahweh has taken a barbaric cultural ritual and made it much better.

Secondly, the process is controlled. Much of the justice of the time – indeed, many of the suspicions of jealous husbands – was delivered outside of the rule of law. In a male dominated culture, men might well seek their own retribution when they suspected marital unfaithfulness. Yet this trial is conducted in a very specific way before the priest himself. There is no room for personal vengeance.

Thirdly, the regulations are laden with meaning. Words accompany every stage (for example, the oath spoken in verse 21). The washing of the words from the scroll into the water is an obvious sign to the participants as to what is going on. The Lord is concerned for purity in marriage and adultery cannot be accepted.

So, though it may at first appear like a Middle Ages witch trial, this section is actually quite different. The preacher or teacher will probably have to explain these differences to a congregation or Bible study group as this is one of those issues where wrong ideas will prevent listeners from hearing much else (and this passage is sometimes quoted by Bible opponents as an example of the Bible's irrelevance).

Working through the text in a little more detail, we can see that the basic approach is for the couple to go to the priest (moral issues are always spiritual issues), present an offering, wait for the drink to be prepared and then, once taken, the effect of the drink will determine the guilt of the woman. It is interesting to see that the priest is the one who supervises the trial. The judges (established by Moses in Exodus 18 at the suggestion of his father-in-law) presumably try civil cases. The question of adultery, however, goes right to the heart of the moral and spiritual life of Israel and so must be brought before the priest.

The introductory comments (5:11-14) establish the circumstances in which the trial applies. It concerns the situation where a jealous husband suspects (but cannot prove) some infidelity. Early on in the text there is a suggestion that the fault may well lie with the husband rather than the wife as he may suspect her 'even though she is not impure.' Again, we see a more compassionate kind of justice than the contemporary world of the time, where the husband's suspicions were often enough to bring punishment against a wife. The husband presents his wife to the priest with an offering (5:15) for 'jealousy'. It is not immediately clear what purpose this offering serves, though it is an integral part of the trial (see verses 18 and 25). Most likely the offering is to recognise that the husband's suspicions may be unfounded. Alternatively, the function of the jealousy offering may be to protect the woman who is in great danger as she 'comes near' (vv. 16 and 18).

Verse 16 is important as it establishes that the woman, whilst physically standing in the priest's presence, is in fact to 'stand before the Lord'. This phrase is repeated in verses 18 and in the summary in verse 30. The reader should be in no doubt that the justice will be overseen by Yahweh himself.

The actual process of the trial involves water mixed with dust from the tabernacle floor (v. 17, it is this which makes it holy) and the words of the oath washed off the scroll (v. 23) and into the water. The priest then speaks the words of the oath (vv. 19-22) which includes a wasting curse which implies that a guilty woman will not be able to bear any children. In English the first part of the curse seems to imply pregnancy ('your abdomen swells') but this would be a strange consequence, especially as the second part of the curse is that 'your thighs waste away.' Taken together the two implications strongly infer that the guilty woman will not be able to conceive.

Leviticus 20:10 mandates stoning as a punishment for adultery. Some commentators see this as contradictory to Numbers 5. However, as verse 13 makes clear, this particular set of regulations covers the situation where there are no witnesses, without whom a death sentence cannot be pronounced (see also Numbers 35:30).

The accused woman must agree to the trial saying, 'Amen. So be it' (v. 22) establishing yet another difference with the unfair trials which forced a woman to participate whether or not she was willing. Here, her participation is voluntary. The writing of the oath and the washing of the words into the water (vv. 23-24) are clearly a very graphic illustration of the process.

Sceptics point out that there is no evidence that this regulation was ever enacted in ancient Israel, but that is hardly the point. Its very nature is a last chance approach where the normal courses of trial and restitution (like those of 5:5-10) have been exhausted, so we would expect it to be enacted only rarely.

Purity in service (6:1-21)
Chapter 6 appears to be quite a leap from the sordid world of adultery and jealousy. However, as noted above, the

same theme of purity and the same introductory formula 'The Lord said' joins the passages together. The Nazirite regulations are remarkable for two reasons.

+ This is the first instance of voluntary service in Numbers. Up to now all service has been by conscription, whether it is the fighting armies counted in chapter 1 or the various clans of Levi tasked with transporting the tabernacle in chapters 3 and 4. Now, however, provision is made for the Israelites who choose to set themselves apart for service.

+ The second surprise is that this procedure is available to both men and women (v. 2). Even though all the subsequent references are masculine (and it is not clear how some of the hair cutting regulations might apply to a female) the service vow is non-discriminatory, available to all of Israel.

Some scholars consider this section to be a later addition because the Bible evidence is that Nazirite vows were for life – like those relating to Samson (Judges 13) or Samuel (1 Samuel 1). But it is better to go with the Bible's chronology and see the cases of Samson and Samuel as special cases of a more general principle; namely that any Israelite could set him or herself apart for service to Yahweh for a particular task or time.

In such a case the dedication to the task must be total. The repetition of the phrase 'all the days' (ESV) is lost in the NIV translation ('as long as' and 'throughout the period'). It occurs in verses 4, 5, 6 and 8. The message is clear – any man or woman who gives themselves to voluntary service must do it wholeheartedly. The passage deals with the practicalities of this setting apart – he or she is not, for example, to go near a dead body, even a close relative (vv. 6-8). In fact, if a Nazirite comes across a dead body by accident (for example if someone dies in their presence – not unthinkable!) then the period of dedication must begin all over again (vv. 9-12).

Importantly, there is also provision for the end of service (vv. 13-20). The ceremonies at the Tent of Meeting centre on the offerings that must be made (sin, burnt and fellowship). Despite all the careful avoidance of anything unclean during the whole tenure of his service, the Nazirite still needs to go through the entire panoply of sacrifices. There is a hint here that perfect purity can be striven for but never attained (no one is holier than the Nazirite) – sacrifice will always be needed, even for the apparently 'consecrated' man or woman.

Traditionally, Christians have made much of the Nazirites abstention from alcohol (v. 4) but even a cursory reading shows that this is a misapplication. Those who take such a view rarely apply the other rules (for example, not cutting hair) and the fast is not just from alcohol but from 'anything that comes from the grapevine, not even the seeds or the skin.' Wine and fruit from the vine were part of everyday culture and the Nazirite sets himself apart from the norms of everyday life. His holiness is evident not in tee-total abstention but in making sure he is untainted by the world.

The Lord's response (6:22-27)

The priestly blessing in the last verses of chapter 6 is relatively well known. It is probably an expansion of Leviticus 9:22 which mentions a priestly blessing in passing but gives no detail. Although many English Bibles subtitle the section 'priestly blessing' or 'Aaron's blessing' the words make clear that this is actually a blessing from Yahweh himself given through the high priest.

The blessing itself sits nicely in the context. God has set out the order and arrangement of the fighting camp and spoken to his people through Moses about the need for purity in all walks of life. Now he speaks a word of blessing. For 'if you fully obey the Lord your God and carefully follow all his commands I give you today, the Lord your God will set you high above all the nations on earth. All these blessings will come upon you and accompany you if you obey the Lord your God' (Deut. 28.1-2). The blessings of the covenant come to those who obey the covenant and are pure. Therefore, whilst it is tempting for the preacher to take a rich text out of its immediate context, it is strongly connected to what precedes and follows.

+ The heart of the blessing is putting the Lord's name on the Israelites (v. 27) which will lead to their being blessed. The idea of having God's name is expanded in some of the vocabulary used as part of the blessing.

+ To 'keep' (v. 24) is a very broad idea indeed. It incorporates watching and guarding as well as protection.

+ Verses 25 and 26 are a little less poetic in Hebrew than in English where the same Hebrew word *pn* is translated as both 'face' and 'countenance' (a throwback to the King James Version). Whilst we might argue on linguistic grounds that such a translation is unnecessary, we can hardly argue that such an exalted blessing does not deserve such poetic language. However, the sense of the first part of both verses is the same (that God would look upon his people) – the parallelism is found in the second part of each line: verse 25 offers the grace of God whilst verse 26 offers his peace.

+ The language of grace is interesting here. Even though the blessings of the Old Covenant are in some way dependent upon observance of the law, there is still recognition, even within the blessing itself, that God's grace is necessary for the people to journey successfully (a point well made by the unfolding story of Numbers).

From text to message

Getting the message clear: the theme

Rooted in the Old Covenant, it is clear that a holy Lord wants his people to be holy too. This includes how they relate to him, how they relate to one another and even how they serve him. Even when they fail he provides a way for sin to be addressed.

Getting the purpose clear: the aim

Yahweh wants his people to know how to live pure lives and to understand that sin must be atoned for. The passage, therefore, contains both demand and grace. The preacher or Bible teacher must keep these two tensions in mind. On the one hand there is a clear call to live in a way that pleases our Lord. On the other, we need a realistic view of sin and confidence that in Christ there is both forgiveness and power to say no to ungodliness.

A way in

A sermon or Bible study on holiness could be very dry. However, Numbers gives us the setting of a journey and we will be true to the context if we build on this picture. For example, there are many ways to get from London to Birmingham and someone who is waiting for us in

Birmingham might not mind that much which route
we have taken. But Scripture does not present our God
as a distant relative awaiting our arrival. He is our near
companion, with us every step of the way and present in
the church (the 'camp'). Therefore it matters to him how
we travel. This illustration could no doubt be developed
further.

Alternatively, the preacher could make much of the
markers found at the start of each section. How do we
know what is important to God? We might have many
ideas? Church organisation, music style, whom we should
marry and so on. But the real test is what does God say?
If I am really concerned about something, I will speak up.
Most people do. When God speaks up, his people have to
listen.

Ideas for application

+ God's call to purity is both private and corporate and,
  in both cases, lived out before him.

+ God's desire for his people to be pure stems from his
  own purity and presence. However, he recognises that
  we cannot attain purity and so provides atonement for
  sin in Christ Jesus.

+ Sin always has both vertical and horizontal elements
  and we must address both when we slip into
  wrongdoing. Jesus pays the penalty for our sin, but
  that does not excuse us from making good with our
  wronged brother or sister.

+ Marriage is especially important as it is a picture of
  Christ and the church. Therefore we must pray for
  and seek strong marriages, confessing our corporate

sin when things do not go right and rejoicing together at marriages of longevity and strength.

+ God calls all people to serve him wholeheartedly. This means to be sacrificial, focused and dedicated – whilst also being realistic about our remaining sinful nature.

+ As with all the stories in Numbers, we feel the tension between salvation accomplished and salvation completed. We must not presume on what God has done for us in the past, but 'make every effort to enter that rest' as Hebrews 4:11 puts it.

+ We enjoy the promised blessings of God in Christ. He has perfectly fulfilled the law and lived a pure life of righteousness for us.

Suggestions for preaching

Sermon 1

If preaching the whole section, the focus must be on purity. The Lord is concerned for this at every level and strata of society – corporate and personal. Indeed the refrain 'be holy as I am holy' forms a bedrock for both Old Covenant obedience (Lev. 19) and New Covenant living (1 Pet. 1:16). In this sense, it is important to see purity as a positive not a negative: it is not just "do not", but more fundamentally "do", i.e. "be like Yahweh."

However, the Bible is also realistic and recognises that things can and do go wrong. Our journey is captured perfectly by the book of Numbers, midway between salvation accomplished and salvation realised. Along the way purity is not a given, but something to strive for.

One sermon might be about the need for purity amongst
God's people. To use the language of 1 Peter, Christians
must not 'conform to the evil desires' we had 'when we lived in
ignorance' but 'be holy.' This section of Numbers shows us why:

+ **The Lord is holy**: he dwells in the camp and therefore
  uncleanness defiles the camp. Anyone who wrongs
  another actually wrongs him (5:6). The suspected wife
  must be brought before the Lord and her case is not
  settled by the civil judges but before the priest. The
  Nazirite must consecrate himself to the Lord (6:2,
  5). However, the holiness of God is not enough of
  a motivation for our holiness. I can support a football
  team of great and talented players, but I do not need
  to be talented myself, I can just watch from a distance.
  God's demands affect all his people, because:

+ **The Lord is present**: all through this section Yahweh
  makes clear he is near. He is especially present in the
  camp. He is affected by sin between two individuals.
  The adultery test is brought right into the place where
  he dwells. The same nearness of God is used by Paul as
  a motivation for purity using the language of the temple
  both corporately (1 Cor. 3:16) and for individuals
  (1 Cor. 6:19). The same emphasis on both corporate
  and individual purity is seen here in Numbers.

+ **The Lord is concerned**. Numbers 5–6 paints a picture
  of a God who is concerned for how we journey to the
  promised land. He primarily expresses this concern
  through the markers which occur at the beginning
  of each section, 'The Lord said…' If something is
  important it needs to be said, and God speaks here
  about what concerns him.

- **The Lord is gracious.** Whilst blessing under the Old Covenant is not to be considered separately from obedience, it is clear from the final doxology of this passage that God's grace still drives the covenant relationship. The people have been rescued because of his intervention and the law under which they operate is given as a response to his grace. It is fitting, therefore, that the section ends (6:22-27) with a focus on the gracious nature of Yahweh towards his people.

Such a sermon would need to be realistic about sin (as the text is) and recognise there is still need for reconciliation and forgiveness (clearly seen in 5:5-10, but also in 6:13-20), both horizontal (between men) and vertical (man to God). Such purity means we can enjoy God's blessings (6:22-27). Not only is our purity ultimately found in Christ; his obedience to his Father means that, in him, we can enjoy the blessings of a gracious Father. Striving for purity is not about law keeping, but walking closely with Christ in the power of his Spirit who lives within us.

Sermon 2

Another sermon might focus more on the detail of the passages, perhaps breaking up the sections a little more. Chapter 5 is generally negative (what to do when something goes wrong). Chapter 6 is generally more positive (holy service) and these could be taken separately.

A sermon on chapter 5 might stress the need for holiness:

- in our corporate walk before God (5:1-4)

- in our lives shared with each other (5:5-10)

- in the most intimate of relationships (5:11-31)

The preacher will have to be careful not to preach the 'letter written on stone tablets' (2 Cor. 3:3) for that 'letter kills' (2 Cor. 3:6). However, such an approach will emphasise that Christianity is an all or nothing calling and that God longs for purity in every area of our lives. The line to Christ will be similar to that shown above.

Sermon 3

A sermon on chapter 6 might be more positive in outlook. The call to service like that of the Nazirite belongs to the Old Covenant law. Nevertheless there are principles that can be drawn as we serve God (a calling for every believer). The passage contains strong themes of sacrifice, dedication, focus and realism. Lest this sound somewhat like a self-help programme, we should remind listeners that the ultimate Nazirite is Christ himself – not necessarily in fulfilling the absolute requirements of Numbers 6, but in the way he 'endured the cross, scorning its shame.' He gave himself willingly for our purity and would not be distracted from his great task.

Suggestions for teaching

Questions to help understand the passage

1. Why must unclean people be sent outside the camp (5:3)? What does this imply about the character of the Lord?

2. How is sin understood in 5:6 (compare Psalm 51:3-4)? How does such an understanding of sin help us relate to God?

3. How does the section 5:5-10 show how both the horizontal (people to people) and vertical (people to God) effects of sin are dealt with?

4. Why is restitution (5:7) necessary?

5. What is the Lord's main concern in 5:11-31? Why? What other Scriptures take the issue of marital faithfulness seriously like this one?

6. Why do the possibly sinful couple have to come to the priest and not the judges Moses sets up in Exodus 18?

7. There is little in chapter 6 about what a Nazirite actually does or how he/she fulfils their vow. What, instead, is the focus? Why is this?

8. Why are sacrifices necessary at the end of a Nazirite's vow (6:13-21)?

9. How is the blessing of 6:22-27 connected to the Lord's demands for purity?

Questions to help apply the passage

1. What does the Lord's demand for absolute purity tell us about our own journey through the wilderness?

2. How does the coming of Christ and the presence of his Spirit in the church shape what we read in 5:1-4?

3. What kinds of issues does the New Testament identify as being unworthy of God's holy people?

4. How might the principles behind confession and restitution (5:5-10) work in the church today?

5. Why must God's people have a high view of marriage (see also Ephesians 5:25-33)?

6. What do some of the principles of service set out in chapter 6 tell us about our own service? How do they, ultimately, point to the great servant, Jesus Christ?

7. How do Christians go about enjoying God's blessing
    today? (Refer to Ephesians 1:3-4 for guidance).

3
WORSHIP (7–8)

Introduction

Chapters 7 and 8 seem at first glance to be out of place in the book. They do not appear in chronological order: the introductory statement 'When Moses had finished setting up the tabernacle...' takes us back to Exodus 40:17. They also seem out of place because the previous section (Aaron's blessing) seems to end the law-giving section and we feel ready for the departure story, a sort of "let's get on with it!"

Why, then, is this section here? Some commentators identify that it completes a long legal section which began in Leviticus 1 and has progressed through to Numbers 6. More likely, it is not until the duties of priests and Levites (in both Leviticus and Numbers) have been outlined that the consecration of the tabernacle makes sense. Either way, chapters 7 and 8 take us back before the census of chapter 1.

The most important verse in this section is 7:89 which explains, using repetition, the exact focus of the tabernacle – it is primarily the place where God speaks to Moses (as opposed to the place where sacrifices are offered, though this too is part of its function). We see this emphasis clearly: 'When Moses entered the Tent of Meeting to *speak* with the Lord, he heard the voice *speaking* to him from between the two cherubim above the atonement cover on the ark of the Testimony. And he *spoke* with him' (my italics added for emphasis). The sacrifices are a means to an end – the end is the relationship with a God who speaks.

So, the lines of communication are open. Truly now, the people are ready for their journey.

Listening to the text

Context and structure

After the detail of the offerings in chapter 7 (which is narrative rather than law), there follow three sections all introduced with the formula, 'The Lord said...' Thus the chapters have this shape:

- Complete list of offerings for the tabernacle consecration (7:1-89)

- Laws to do with the tabernacle operation:
  - The seven lamps (8:1-4)
  - The Levites (8:5-22)
  - Levite retirement (8:23-26)

Initially, there seems to be little connection between the first section with its concluding emphasis on hearing God's voice and the later sections. We will try to see how the various components fit together as we progress through the text.

Working through the text

Complete list of offerings for the tabernacle consecration (7:1-89)

Throughout this passage the two titles 'tabernacle' and 'Tent of Meeting' are used interchangeably. They are not, as some commentators seem to think, two separate structures, but one and the same. Tabernacle refers to a more general description and is not capitalised by the NIV (or the ESV). 'Tent of Meeting' is a more exact title and it is capitalised by most English translations. Exodus 28:43 confirms that these are the same structure using the title 'Tent of Meeting' for a place that is obviously the tabernacle with its altar and Holy Place.

The list of offerings begins with an introductory section in verses 1 to 9. After some opening statements about the consecration the emphasis seems to be on the wagons that were brought as part of the offering. Each tribe seems to have joined together with another and provided one cart per two tribes (v. 3). In addition, each tribe provides an ox.

These are then distributed to the three Levite clans according to their roles. The Kohathites receive none for they have to carry the holy objects by hand (v. 9). The Gershonites receive just two for their load is the lighter soft furnishings (see chapters 3 and 4). The Merarites, however, who have the responsibility for carrying poles, scaffolding and so on receive four for these weightier items.

These transport details may, at first, seem to be rather inconsequential. However, not only do they support the section that follows (where each tribe brings an equal offering), they play an important part in the history of the Ark of the Covenant, explaining, as they do, a rather obscure incident in the reign of King David (2 Sam. 6).

There, the Ark is being brought back to Jerusalem by David from the house of Abinadab where it has resided since being regained from the Philistines. The Israelites place the Ark on a new cart (there is some sense in which they are trying to do what is right) to bring it to its rightful home. But, 'when they came to the threshing floor of Nacon, Uzzah reached out and took hold of the ark of God, because the oxen stumbled. The Lord's anger burned against Uzzah because of his irreverent act; therefore God struck him down and he died there beside the ark of God' (2 Sam. 6.6-7).

This incident hardly makes sense unless read in the light of Numbers 7. The ark is *not* to be carried on a cart, even a new one. The Kohathites were given no carts for either the ark nor the other holy objects – they had to be carried by hand. This explains the anger of the Lord against Uzzah. Numbers explains that when the tabernacle was dismantled, everything was covered up – nothing *could* be touched (see Numbers 4:5-6).

After the gifts of the carts and oxen, each tribe brings its offering for the dedication. At this point some contemporary translations do the text a great disservice by summarising it in one or two paragraphs with this kind of formula: 'these are the days, these are the leaders, and they all brought this.'[1] True, this is 'one of the most repetitive and, consequently, one of the most ignored passages in the OT'.[2] However, as Ashley points out, it serves a very important purpose. 'The author wanted the cumulative effect that results from a reading of the account of twelve identical offerings…each

---

1   Notably the *Living Bible*, *The Contemporary English Version*, *Today's English Version* (*The Good News Bible*) and *The New Century Version* (also published as *The Youth Bible*). All of these are, in many respects, fine translations.

2   Ashley, p. 161

tribe had an equal stake in the support of the sacrificial ministry of the tabernacle. No tribe has a monopoly…and no tribe is unnecessary.'[3] Or, as Duguid puts it, 'here was an overwhelming outpouring of love on the part of each and every one of the tribes of Israel that cannot be captured in a few words or phrases. Only a full rendition of the details will give an adequate sense of what is transpiring here.'[4] These are glorious principles from such an unpromising passage!

Each tribal offering is outlined in a parallel paragraph. The day, leader and tribe are named followed by the offering formula:

- A grain offering made up of a silver plate, bowl and dish (or more likely spoon), the first two filled with flour and oil

- A burnt offering consisting of one young bull, one ram and one one-year old male lamb

- A sin offering, namely a male goat

- A fellowship offering made up of 2 oxen and five each of rams, male goats and male lambs.

Note the completeness of the contributions, covering all the major Levitical offerings.

This section is brought to an appropriate climax in verse 89 which, as we have already seen, emphasises the communicative role that the tabernacle is to play in the life of Israel. It is not simply the place where these contributions are offered, but the place where relationship is maintained

---

3   Ashley, p. 164
4   Duguid, p. 97

with Yahweh which ultimately means the place where he *speaks* (see Exodus 25:22). The 'mercy seat' is also called the atonement cover and takes us directly to Christ, who is himself described in the New Testament using exactly the same phrase from the Greek version of the Old Testament. 'God presented him as a *sacrifice of atonement* [mercy seat] through faith in his blood, to demonstrate his righteousness' (Rom. 3:25).

The seven lamps (8:1-4)
It is not immediately clear why the author should move to the question of the lamps next. The lamps are described in greater detail in Exodus 25 and 37. No other tabernacle furnishings are expanded upon here. Perhaps it is the perfect nature of the seven-lamped stand that causes comment? Perhaps, as one commentator has suggested, it is because this is the first item Moses would have seen?

More likely, it is the question of what the lampstands are for that solicits attention. They are to 'light the area in front of the lampstand.' This is the way through to the Most Holy Place where Yahweh will speak with Moses. On this reading the lampstand aids the communion with God that Moses must seek. Remember there is no chapter division in the Hebrew and this would seem to be the most natural reading.

The Levites (8:5-22)
The next section picks up on some earlier themes which explain that the Levites are substitutionary servants set apart for service at the tabernacle. Although it bears similarities to Leviticus 8 there are some significant differences. The Leviticus passage deals with priests – those who are holy or consecrated (Lev. 8:12). Their status allows them to serve at the altar. The Levites described here have a lesser

status – 'purified' (v. 7) which allows them to do the work of guarding and carrying.

Some commentators see a very complex chiasm here which may be possible. Even without such a structure, it is fairly obvious to the reader that the purification of the Levites involves their cleansing (v. 12) so that they can belong to the Lord. Their work at the tent is also described as being a gift to Aaron (v. 19). The passage sees no contradiction between the Levites being for both Aaron and the Lord, just as, for example, tithes are offerings given to God but collected by the Levites. It is clear that the Levites are not able to serve without this colourful ceremony. Approaching the tent, even at a distance, is a serious and dangerous business.

There are one or two perplexing details in the passage. It is not clear, for example, why the Levites have to shave their whole bodies (v. 7). We simply cannot say what the significance of this action is, though it also occurs in Leviticus 14:8-9. It clearly plays some part in ritual cleansing. Similarly, the laying on of hands (v. 10 and then verse 12) is almost certainly a substitutionary sign that the Levites are living sacrifices.

Levite retirement (8:23-26)
The passage concludes with a short retirement section which we have already discussed (see notes on 3:40-51). Levites are not expected to do long hard manual labour for all their years, though old age does not preclude them from guard duty.

This small insert concludes the readiness of the tabernacle and its servants. It could easily have been placed elsewhere in the text, but its place here gives some dynamism and movement to an otherwise historically static passage. The Levite service is an ongoing thing, just as the covenant will continue. The set-up and consecration may be one off events marking the beginning of the sacrificial life of Israel, but as time goes on, Levites will grow old and retire. They will, presumably, be replaced by younger servants, those babies a month old or more who were counted at 3:39.

From text to message

Getting the message clear: the theme

Setting up the tabernacle is the final significant event before the journey can begin. Everyone plays their part and none is left out. All the preparations point to one eternal truth, that 'there was fellowship between God and his people, accomplishing the goal of the covenant in every age and generation.'[5] And how is this fellowship best expressed? – through God's people hearing his voice. 'And the Lord said...' is more, therefore, than a good title. It is at the heart of covenant relationship with our living God.

Getting the message clear: the aim

Christians, just as Old Testament believers, need to see the importance of coming to God *together* our sin dealt with, so that we can hear the voice of God. Both of these are achieved through Christ who opens a new and living way to God and is, supremely, the Word of God.

A way in

What change did the Reformers make to church architecture? They changed churches so that rather than an altar, a pulpit was front centre in their buildings. What was at the heart of the tabernacle? It was the ark of the covenant. The tabernacle was, at its heart, not a place of sacrifice (the altar), but a place of relationship where God spoke. That's why the tabernacle is also called the Tent of Meeting, not

---

5   Duguid, p. 101

just where Israelites met each other, but where they met God. This was at the heart of their worship.

An alternative approach is to use the story of Uzzah to create some narrative tension and then drop the bomb shell of his demise. It matters to God how people come to him.

Ideas for application

+ There is a strong application of the corporate nature of worship seen in these chapters. Each of the tribes has a part to play.

+ The operation of the covenant is clear. Sacrifices have to be brought so that Yahweh can be approached. The essence of his relationship is that he then speaks to his people.

+ The sacrifices are a clear and costly reminder that Yahweh cannot be approached casually. Sin must be dealt with.

+ There is also a strong application about service. Whilst the Levites do not translate directly into New Covenant terms, we are a 'kingdom of priests'.

+ Christ's only sacrifice on the cross stands at the heart of the Christian message; however it is important to see it as a means to an end. The end is a living relationship with the triune God that Christ's atoning death makes possible.

Suggestions for preaching

Sermon 1

Using the idea that people cannot just come to God as they please, there are some clear lessons about approaching God – what we might narrowly call 'worship.'

+ **Worship is God-centred.** This is more of an introductory point, already seen in Numbers but reinforced through the way the tribes come to Yahweh.

+ **Worship involves being together** with everyone involved. The passage paints a picture of total involvement by all the people. None is excluded or omitted. See Psalm 122:3-4 for a graphic picture of this unity.

+ **Worship involves sacrificial giving.** This is clear from the offerings made by the tribes. The togetherness and participation of the tribes is expressed in what they give.

+ **Worship requires ministers or leaders.** These are the Levites consecrated in Numbers 8. This is perhaps a weaker point. It is stretching the point to make a direct link from Levites to ministers today, those who ultimately serve the great servant, Christ Jesus. But he has appointed leaders into the church, so there is a comparison to be made. However, the guarding duty is no longer required because of the work of Christ.

+ **Worship must be Bible centred.** The climax of these two chapters comes in Numbers 7:89 when God speaks. It is as though all the preparations have been building to this moment.

Today, it is the work and word of Christ which bring all these ideas together and stand at the heart of our corporate worship.

Sermon 2

Alternatively, and more simply, the covenant relationship between God and his people is expressed in two ways:

+ The people approach God through sacrifice (and, therefore,)

+ The people are sustained by God as he speaks to them

Both of these find their ultimate and lasting fulfilment in Christ Jesus; both are key themes of, for example, the book of Hebrews. This sermon will be simpler but will omit picking up some of the detail of the passage.

Suggestions for teaching

Questions to help understand the passage

1. What is the alternative name for the tabernacle (see 7:4)? What is the significance of this name?

2. What light is shed on the story at the start of 2 Samuel 6 by the descriptions of the oxen and carts?

3. How many of the tribes are involved in bringing the carts and the oxen as offerings (7:1-9)? How many bring other contributions according to the same pattern (7:10-83)?

4. Why does the author represent this long set of data in this way?

5. The climax of the consecration is not sacrifice. What is it (7:89)?

6. Why is the lampstand the only item of tabernacle furniture mentioned (8:1-4)?

7. Read through the purification of the Levites (8:5-22). Whom are they to serve? Why is the ceremony needed?

8. Why is a little section on retirement included here (8:23-26)? What does it add to our understanding?

Questions to help apply the passage

1. What do we learn about approaching God from:

    +   The comprehensive list of tribes?

    +   The gifts and contributions they brought?

        Apply these truths to church life today.

2. If the climax of the consecration is God speaking, how do we ensure we maintain the same focus in our worship?

3. Why are the guarding Levites no longer required in the New Covenant? Look up Hebrews 12:18-24 for help.

4. How does the work and word of Christ satisfy all the requirements and details of Numbers 7–8?

4
Preparation (9–10)

Introduction

Chapters 9 and 10 of Numbers describe the final piece of preparation before the Israelites actually set off. Fittingly, for the final incident at Sinai, the text describes the second Passover and the first to take place subsequent to the Exodus (the first, Exodus 12, precedes the nation's departure). Here we also discover the way that the Israelites will be guided in the wilderness and some practical arrangements for calling them together and giving them marching orders.

There is a thread of anticipation running through this section. As we shall see in just a moment, many of the provisions are temporary, or at least look forward to a time when the people will be settled in the land. Thus there is an expectation and certainty of final arrival already present, even before the journey proper has begun.

However the preacher decides to divide Numbers (whether *geographically* or *spiritually*, see page 25), the end of chapter 10 marks the end of a significant section.

Geographically, the action now moves on from Sinai. Spiritually, the positive view we have of the nation will soon disappear as the rebellions begin almost straight away.

Listening to the text

Context and structure
The passage divides obviously into four (represented by the section headings in most English translations):

+ The second Passover (9:1-14)

+ Guidance for travel (9:15-23)

+ The silver trumpets (10:1-10)

+ Setting out on the journey (10:11-36)

We shall consider each of these sections in turn.

Working through the text

The second Passover (9:1-14)
The first Passover takes place in Egypt itself (see Exodus 12) and is a protection against the tenth and most devastating of the plagues, the death of the firstborn. It is not to be a one off event: 'This is a day you are to commemorate; for the generations to come you shall celebrate it as a festival to the Lord – a lasting ordinance' (Exod. 12:14). Its place here is appropriate. The event which brought the people out of Egypt was the first Passover; likewise the second Passover marks their departure for their final destination – Canaan.

One year on, it is time for Passover again, as the Lord himself reminds Moses (9:1-3). The date stamp in verse 1 puts us back one month before the beginning of the book (1:1). So, chronologically, the actual Passover (v. 4) is celebrated 14 days before the census of chapter 1. However, this is not just a description of another festival; hence its inclusion in the material at this point.

The description in the first few verses of chapter 9 contains some new case law for those who are unclean (9:6-8) and for those absent on a journey (9:9-13). It is worth looking to see how these two extra pieces of law have arisen.

First, the question of those who are unclean is raised by the people. There are certain men (v. 6) who are unable to participate because of uncleanness. Since the first Passover, Moses has been presented with a whole host of regulations to do with ceremonial purity, many of which are recorded in Leviticus, but some in Numbers itself (e.g. Numbers 5–6).

There is a real problem. Some men are unclean through touching a dead body. Such an eventuality is inevitable. In a population of over 2 million, people will die every day and dead bodies have to be disposed of. But those who do so will find themselves unable to take part in the Passover, that most significant and poignant of remembrance meals. What is to happen?

Moses clearly agrees that this is an important question and so he brings the case before the Lord. However, the Lord addresses not only this question but another further question which does not seem to have struck Moses or the Israelites just yet. What about those who are away from home on a journey? At first this seems an unrelated question. What has uncleanness got to do with travelling absence? And why would Israelites be absent from the marching column anyway?

The answer is that they would *not be* absent, why would they be? This is a provision for a *settled* people. Settled people go on journeys and are absent from home. It's not a situation that's going to arise in the desert. Moreover the instructions for the alien are only marginally relevant to the travelling generation. There were already instructions for the inclusion of non-Israelites (see Exodus 12:48-49). Now these are explained more explicitly. Once again, these rules probably have more significance to a settled generation.

The penalties for non-participation seem, at first, somewhat severe (9:13). But it should be remembered that the penalty for not participating in the first Passover was equally final: suffering the consequence of the tenth plague.

Thus the Passover rules begin to reflect a new reality: Israel is not simply a rescued people, they will be a people with an identity and a land to inhabit. The Promised Land is in sight!

Guidance for travel (9:15-23)
How, though, are the people to know when to travel? Careful readers of this era of history will know that the Lord has already demonstrated his guiding hand (see, for example Exodus 13:17 when he leads the Israelites away from the Philistines). Now the explanation of how God is to lead is explained in more detail. It is directly linked to his presence among his people – the cloud appears over the top of the tabernacle (here given another name, the Tent of Testimony). The cloud appears as fire at night, cloud by day and thus easy to see.

Although the cloud is described in one place as being for guidance (Exod. 13:21), this is not its normal function. Elsewhere in Exodus and here in Numbers it is to be the way that the people would know *when* to set out. In practical terms this makes sense. In marching order the tabernacle is to be carried in the centre of the marching line (2:17). It can hardly be an early form of Sat-Nav if half of the people are ahead of it.

Thus, the question of how the people were guided is not answered and it is important not to impose on the text something it does not say. Numbers 9 is very clearly about knowing when to set up camp and when to break camp.

There is something else about the camp that the preacher or teacher should notice. There is a refrain that runs through it – 'at the Lord's command' appearing 9 times in its various forms. Some commentators even think this is a form of early hymn or travelling song – just as English sailors would sing shanties as they weighed anchor or prepared for battle, so here is the Israelites' camping song, 'at the Lord's command.'

Perhaps that idea is a bit speculative. It nonetheless raises the profile of the refrain which will be sadly absent as soon as the journey begins.

The silver trumpets (10:1-10)
The trumpets, initially at least, fulfil an associated purpose. They are made at the Lord's command and they serve two roles: calling people to assembly and announcing the break of camp. The first of these roles is subdivided into two – one trumpet announces 'leaders only' (v. 4). Both trumpets together mean "all hands on deck" (to borrow a nautical phrase). We must presume that the two trumpets had different tones.

For breaking camp there are arrangements to make sure everything works from a practical point of view. A different signal gathers the assembly together (v. 7). It all seems rather ordinary and functional.

The surprise comes in verses 8 to 10 for, like the Passover rules, these trumpets are to have a function once the people have entered the promised land. First, they are a battle signal (v. 9). Just as the census is military in its object (ch. 1) so the trumpets show the people that they are not about to walk into an empty Eden.

Secondly, the trumpets have a ceremonial function – being sounded at feasts, festivals and offerings (v. 10). They thus function as a 'memorial for you before your God' – a future reminder of these travelling days. When the trumpets are sounded at, say, the Firstfruits festival, people will say, "those trumpets date from when we were just setting off." In other words, they will serve as a memorial of what God has done in the past.

They will also, of course, build expectation now. So when a young boy in a small tribe hears the trumpet for breaking camp, his parents can say to him, "Son, one day you will hear that trumpet in our own land."

Setting out on the journey (10:11-36)

The scene is now set for the journey to begin and it happens on the twentieth day of the month when the census is taken (compare 10:11 with 1:1). Verse 12 is a summary verse because the wilderness of Paran camp site is not actually reached until 12:16; before that there is a whole lot of grumbling to contend with at Taberah (11:1-3), Kibroth Hattaavah (11:4-35) and Hazeroth (12:1-15). The pattern of movement shows that the instructions of the previous chapters are being taken seriously. The only slight variation or addition is the detail that the actual tent was set up before those carrying the furnishings (the Kohathites) arrived at the camp site (see 10:17 and 10:21).

It is at this point that Moses' father-in-law makes a reappearance. We last met Jethro giving some very practical advice about judges in Exodus 18. Here, in verse 29-32, he suggests to Moses that he might now leave and return to his own country. Moses begs him to stay. Although we are not told the outcome of the discussion here, the list of descendants in Judges 1:16 implies that Moses' persuasive skills were up to the mark.

One difficult textual question arises at this point. Is Jethro (Exod. 18) the same man as Reuel (Exod. 2:16-18 and here) or Hobab (Reuel's son here, also Judges 4:11)? The apparent discrepancy is best explained by the fact that the Hebrew word *hoten* has a wider meaning than "father-in-law", perhaps more accurately reflecting the colloquial term we would use today "in-laws." On this basis, Jethro (second name Reuel) is the father of Moses' wife and Hobab her brother.

The question of how exactly the cloud and fire gives direction is now answered because the ark is detached from the marching column (v. 33-34) to settle a camping location.

Finally in this section we are told of the short song that Moses sang as the ark moved and as it settled. Both times we are clear that the key issue is the presence of Yahweh with his people, the 'countless thousands of Israel' (the NIV captures the idiom well).

From text to message

Getting the message clear: the theme
The key idea coursing through these sections is that everything is to be done at the Lord's command. He will lead his people to their promised land as their rescuer, just as he brought them out of Egypt. A second, but important, idea is that we begin now to see into the future: God's rules include provisions for when the people are settled in Canaan.

Getting the message clear: the aim

As Christians journey to their own promised land they must also see that they are following Christ there and so they must give themselves to him. He is the one who has rescued us and he is the one who will bring us home.

A way in

Before you set off on a long journey or flight, there are certain preparations you must make. The British Airways website contains helpful lists of things to think about: how to avoid illness; what medicines to pack; what size of luggage you are allowed; what documents you need; what to drink and so on. If you want to arrive at your destination in good health (or even, at all), you would do well to listen to this advice. Similarly as Christians travelling with Christ our Rock to the heavenly city we need to make adequate preparations for our journey.

A more humorous example is that of the story of marathon runner Rob Sloan who was disqualified from his medal place after it emerged that he had travelled at least some of the way on a bus. The story was reported by the BBC in October 2011.[1]

Ideas for application

+ God's plan for journeying is that people should look both backwards (remembrance) and forwards (anticipation). The backwards look is especially to the salvation event; in the New Covenant this is, of course, the cross.

---

1   http://www.bbc.co.uk/news/uk-england-tyne-15252687, accessed 20 September 2012

+ The trumpets are a reminder that the journey has a battle element, but the nature of the calls reinforce the corporate rather than the individual nature of this battle.

+ The 'command' refrain shows that the faith to which God calls us has fruit – the fruit of obedience (see, for example, Romans 1:5).

+ Once again, it is important to remember that Christ journeyed with the Israelites and his own presence by his Spirit on our journey brings these lessons into sharp focus.

Suggestions for preaching

Sermon 1
One idea for a sermon that picks up on themes from the whole passage focuses on the *direction* of some of the instructions:

+ **Don't forget where you have come from** (9:1-14). The Passover is primarily a backward looking meal. The people of Israel were looking forward to Canaan yet needed reminding of their rescue from Egypt and that it was Yahweh himself who brought them out. Though our Lord's Supper is not the Passover meal, Christ *is* our Passover Lamb (1 Cor. 5:7). As we look to the future we cannot hope to travel well unless we remember what Christ has done for us in the past.

+ **Focus on where you are going** (10:1-10). There is no point in being nostalgic. Being an Israelite was not about living in the past, and neither is being a Christian. The trumpets show very clearly that God is giving a certain hope about the Israelites' eventual conquest of the land. There is assurance built-in! Interestingly, the Lord's Supper also does this because it 'proclaims the Lord's death *until he comes*' (1 Cor. 11:26, my italics).

+ **Follow the Lord's commands** (9:15-23). It would be easy to think that in looking backwards and forwards the present does not matter. Far from it! This point could equally apply to the latter part of chapter 10. Everything is done at the Lord's command. The Christian life is a marathon not an orienteering course. In orienteering it doesn't matter how you get from A to B as long as you arrive at B. In a marathon, the runner who does not follow the designated course is disqualified.

Sermon 2

A slower and more detailed approach could easily pick up some of the detail that an outline like that above would necessarily overlook. For example, the trumpets remind us what is at the core of being the people of God:

+ Gathering
+ As whole assembly (10:3)
+ As leaders (10:4)
+ Fighting (10:9)
+ Remembering & celebrating (10:10)

It would be straightforward to see a theology of assembly here which is preserved in the New Covenant but made more real by the work that Christ has done and is doing. There are similar rich themes in the Passover section (9:1-14) and the two travel sections (9:15-23 and 10:11-36).[2]

---

2   For more detailed help and ideas here, see Duguid, p.121-145

Suggestions for teaching

Questions to help understand the passage

1. Why do God's people need to make preparations for the journey to the promised land?

2. Why do you think we learn about the second Passover (9:1-14) here at this point?

3. What question needs resolving (9:6, compare 5:1-4)? What additional issue does the Lord legislate for (9:10) and why?

4. What is the common phrase running through the account of making and breaking camp (9:15-23)?

5. List all the purposes of the silver trumpets (10:1-10). Which of these relate to the journey and which are for the promised land?

Questions to help apply the passage

1. What evidence is there that the Lord expects the Israelites to enter into the land he has promised them?

2. How can they be certain about this? See, for example, Genesis 15:12-14 and 17:8.

3. What makes Christians certain about their ultimate destination?

4. Why does it matter how we travel there? How is this question answered in Numbers?

5. Give thanks for our certain hope (1 Pet. 1:3-9). Pray that we might travel 'at the Lord's command.'

5
DISCONTENT (11–12)

Introduction

There's an immediate change of tone in chapter 11 which will continue (apart from a few gracious interludes) through to the end of the story of the first generation (ch. 25). Now that the journey actually begins (10:33), things go rapidly downhill. The first few verses serve as a general introduction to all the grumbling that will follow. They contain a kind of template of subsequent passages that have more detail: the people grumble; the Lord hears and judges; the people cry out to Moses; Moses intercedes; the Lord relents. All the rebellion passages broadly follow this same pattern.

What is striking about this first round of rebellion is that everyone is affected: it's not just the people, but Moses, Joshua, Miriam and Aaron are all grumblers in some way or another. This murmuring is one of the main negative lessons we are to take from Numbers if we follow Paul's analysis in 1 Corinthians 10:10: 'And do not grumble, as some of them did – and were killed by the destroying angel.'

The preacher must work hard to present the negative picture that is in every part of this story whilst giving a positive exhortation: 'Let us therefore, make every effort to enter that rest, so that no one will fall by following their example of disobedience' (Heb. 4:11). It is always easier to be negative than positive, but faithful preaching is both soberly realistic about the state of the heart and also hugely optimistic about the work of Christ and the sanctification possible by his Holy Spirit.

Listening to the text

Context and structure

The two chapters break down into separate stories of rebellion, though in the case of 11:4-35, the grumbling of the people and Moses is interwoven. For the purposes of this book, we will consider:

+ The first rebellion (11:1-3)

+ The people rebel and Moses doubts (11:4-35)

+ Miriam and Aaron rebel (12:1-16)

However, an alternative way to see the bulk of the section (11:4–12:16) is to see it as the people grappling with two issues – food and leadership. These themes are then intertwined:

+ Food   11:4-9
+ Leadership   11:10-17
+ Food   11:18-23
+ Leadership   11:24-30
+ Food   11:31-34
+ Leadership   12:1-16

Although this helps understand the text, it is unlikely to be a suitable way of preaching the passage as the issues of food and leadership are presenting symptoms of a deeper malaise. Today's issues may be different, but the malaise (unbelief, as identified in Hebrews) will be the same temptation.

Working through the text

The first rebellion (11:1-3)

We know very little about this first bout of grumbling. The exact cause is not clear ('hardships') nor are any ringleaders identified. We know the place name ('Taberah') although this is neither a stopping off point as it is not listed in the summary in 11:35 nor in chapter 33. Probably it stands as a general introduction to this new section which details all the many rebellions to which the people succumb. The verb 'prayed' in verse 2 is only used of Moses in Numbers when he intercedes following one of these incidents.

The people rebel and Moses doubts (11:4-35)

A new section is introduced with a new word to describe the people of God – a 'rabble.' The word is actually a *hapax legomenon*[1] but most translators agree that this is a suitable way of rendering it in English. The NIV renders verse 4 'started wailing' but the ESV is a better translation 'wept again' and makes a link between the two sections.

The Israelites' complaint seems to be that they were better off in Egypt, certainly as far as food is concerned. This will be a theme to which we shall return in later rebellions. Their desire is very strong, 'craved other food' translates 'craved a craving' or 'desired a desire.' It's an extraordinary statement. Whilst we have no way of verifying whether

---

1   A word that only occurs once in Scripture, so there is nothing for translators to compare it to.

they are factually right or not[2], to crave a return to slavery is stupefying! Pharaoh was trying to wipe them out (see Exodus 1:14-16). The exit from Egypt is the nation's salvation: their wish for Egyptian glory-days (even if they ever were) is thus a rejection of what God has done and provided.

Moreover, the manna with which they are so bored is itself a blessing, a gracious provision by a generous God. To reject the manna is therefore to reject the Giver. Moses hears this grumbling, by now spread to every tent (v. 10) and the Lord responds in righteous anger. As yet, we don't know how this will play out because the story is interrupted by an outburst from Moses himself.

Moses' issue is that he cannot look after this grumbling mass of humanity. He sees it as a burden (v. 11) that the Lord has brought upon him. How can he possibly 'carry' them? He sees their problems as ones he must personally solve. Therefore, 'I cannot possibly carry all these people by myself; the burden is too heavy for me.' Remarkably Moses craves death (v. 15) rather than for things to continue as they are. Ironically he desires the very thing the Israelites have left behind in Egypt but now want to return to. Moses' rebellion is now dealt with by God before the issue of the people; Moses is, after all, the appointed mediator.

Yahweh's solution is that, from now on, leadership is going to be shared. This will be demonstrated by some of the Spirit that is on Moses being passed to 70 others. This is more than sharing the administrative burden (as in Exodus 18). The Spirit-anointing shows that spiritual

---

2   Though the delicious spread they describe hardly sounds like fare from the slave-table

leadership is in view. There is no doubt in the context that this refers to God's Spirit, rather than, say, Moses' spirit.

Alongside this promise for leadership help is a promise of meat for the people (vv. 18-20). However, this provision is not to be a gracious blessing (like the manna) but a judgement. Like Romans 1, the people will get what they deeply desire and it will be a stench to them – coming out of their nostrils (v. 20).

Even at this point Moses is not content! Recalling the census, he realises that he could not possibly provide the kind of quantity of meat that the Lord has in mind. He has not yet grasped that, just as the manna came from heaven, so shall the meat. The Lord's rebuke is stinging. 'Is the Lord's arm too short? You will see now whether or not what I say will come true for you' (v. 23).

The 'now' may belong to the first phrase of this sentence: 'Is the Lord's arm too short *now*.' This may make more sense. Moses has seen remarkable things: all ten plagues; the parting of the water; the defeat of the Egyptians; manna from heaven; water from a rock; battle victories; the glory in the tabernacle. A bit of meat hardly seems much trouble for the Almighty. Moses has not learned from what he has experienced in the past and so Yahweh is right to say things have not changed.

The next part of the story shows the fulfilment of God's promise of extra leaders (vv. 24-25, fulfilling vv. 16-17). The prophesying is almost certainly a mark of the Spirit's anointing to show that the transfer had been effective. That is why it did not subsequently continue. The purpose of the transfer is not to produce seventy prophets, but seventy assistant leaders. The prophesying thus stands as evidence that these are appointed from on high to assist Moses.

Two of the chosen seventy, however, do not come to the tent. Their names are Eldad and Medad. We need to be clear that there is no question of this being a negative comment, otherwise the Spirit would not have rested upon them (a positive endorsement). Rather, we must assume that they could not come to the tabernacle for genuine reasons (even though they are unspecified). Moses' young assistant, Joshua doesn't like this situation when he finds out about it and tries to get Moses to halt it.

Moses refuses. 'Are you jealous for my sake? Would that all the Lord's people were prophets, that the Lord would put his Spirit on them!' (v. 29). The problem is solved because, rather than demanding their presence at the tabernacle, Moses and the elders (note, not prophets) return to the camp, where these two are.

Joshua seems also to be infected with the grumbling spirit in the camp. His concern (not unlike Moses at the start of the story) seems to be with Moses' reputation. He is, indeed, jealous for Moses' sake. But by now, Moses has learnt his lesson and realises that Joshua's enthusiasm is misplaced.

The first part of the story is then completed by the description of the quail (not the first time the people have tasted this meat, see Exodus 16). A huge amount is blown in from the sea and caught for eating.[3] No one person gathers less than ten homers. A homer is a measure of volume and may well mean "a donkey-load." Ten homers is thus a lot of poultry! Spread out around the camp, it is no wonder it made people ill. But this illness is more than the first case of salmonella; rather it is a divine judgement. The place name, Kibroth Hattaavah means 'graves of craving' and is entirely apposite.

---

3   Quail is still caught in this area today using nets strung about a metre from the ground. The account thus has a ring of authenticity about it.

One feature missing from this story is Moses' intercession on behalf of the people (which features in nearly every other rebellion narrative and in 11:1-3). We cannot be certain why this is, but it may be that Moses is himself included as part of the judgement of quail. This may also explain why there is no direct judgement against Moses for his rebellion, although it is possible to argue that the taking of 'some of the Spirit' and passing it on is judgement itself.

Miriam and Aaron rebel (12:1-16)
The focus of attention now moves to the inner circle of Moses, Miriam and Aaron. At first this seems like a separate story, but it is connected to the previous sections by a common theme (grumbling) and common concern (leadership). Miriam and Aaron are the sister and brother of Moses respectively, and are probably listed in this order because Miriam is the chief troublemaker.

Their issue presents itself at first as being 'because of [Moses'] Cushite wife, for he had married a Cushite.' This warrants some explanation. We have already met Moses' wife, Zipporah (see Exodus 4:18-26). She seems to have been good for Moses, saving his life before the Lord. However, in that earlier passage she seems to be from Midian, not Cush. Some commentators have rushed to assume a second wife, married around this time, who had incurred the wrath of the siblings.

However, the Hebrew *kus* (Cush) describes a broad area which sometimes accommodates what the Bible writers also call Midian. In later writings they are almost synonyms (see, for example, Habakkuk 3:7). Given that there is no other record of a Cushite wife, it is best to assume that Miriam's and Aaron's complaint is about Zipporah.

But why wait so long? The marriage is quite possibly 40 years old at this point, well established and hardly a cause for concern. We assume that if Yahweh objected, it would have been dealt with by now. Perhaps the sharing of the Spirit (which bypassed Miriam) is the cause for intervention at this point? This theory holds up well, because reading on in verse 2 we get to the real issue which is not about marriage, but about leadership. "'Has the Lord spoken only through Moses?" they asked. "Hasn't he also spoken through us?" And the Lord heard this' (v. 2).

At one level they are correct. Aaron is Moses' prophet (see Exodus 4:15 and 7:1) and as such, though one step removed, he *does* speak the Lord's words. Miriam is also a prophetess (described this way in Exodus 15:20). But the strong implication is that this is a challenge to Moses' leadership, a fact borne out by the Lord's response in verses 6 to 8.

First, though, there is an editorial comment about Moses. It's a strange comment for the author Moses to have made about himself (it would perhaps be self-contradictory?). However, it sets up an expectation that Moses *is* different from Miriam and Aaron, and, indeed, any other leader. This is reinforced by the Lord's reaction. Rather ironically, all three are summoned to the Tent of Meeting from where the Lord speaks. The two siblings saw their leadership credentials as being derived from hearing the Lord's voice: well, they will certainly hear his voice!

The result is two-fold. First, there is a ringing endorsement of Moses' leadership. His relationship with Yahweh is of an altogether different order from that of a prophet. A prophet receives 'visions' and 'dreams.' 'But this is not true of my servant Moses' (v. 7). With Moses, God speaks face to face. Indeed, Moses sees the 'form of the Lord.' The word 'form' (which appears around 10 times in the Old Testament) always means the visible presence of the Lord.

'Face to face' is an idiomatic expression rather than a literal rendering of how Moses approaches Yahweh. We know this because Exodus 33 contains the same expression (Exod. 33:11) whilst holding in tension the statement 'you cannot see my face, for no one may see me and live' (Exod. 33:20).

This should have been enough to warn off Miriam and Aaron. They should have been afraid to 'speak against my servant Moses.' Nor can they plead ignorance. It is clear from Exodus 34:29-35 that all the people knew about this special relationship: 'and when he came out [from the Lord's presence] and told the Israelites what he had been commanded, they saw that his face was radiant.'

The second result of their questioning is judgement against Miriam. It comes in the form of leprosy, a generic term for skin disease. It means that Miriam must go outside the camp. Aaron has to plead with Moses for intercession (again, the text drips with irony!). Moses does so and the sentence is commuted to seven days confinement and disgrace outside the camp – significant enough. There is no doubt that Moses is God's appointed leader.

The lack of judgement against Aaron is perplexing. It may be, as some commentators argue, that Aaron was crucial to the operation of the covenant. There were not, at this point, an army of priests ready to serve, just Aaron and a few direct descendants. More likely, given the order of names in verse 1, Miriam is the chief ringleader and must thus bear the punishment.

From text to message

Getting the message clear: the theme
The overall tone of the passage is downbeat. Rebellion (which here takes the form of grumbling) refuses to

acknowledge either God's power or provision and deserves (and receives) God's judgement.

Getting the message clear: the aim

1 Corinthians is clear: 'do not grumble, as some of them did' (1 Cor. 10:10). This is a negative message, but the Corinthians analysis continues more positively reminding believers that 'God is faithful, he will not let you be tempted beyond what you can bear' (1 Cor. 10:13).

A way in

What do you envy in unbelievers? Money? Car? House? Lifestyle? Coveting is a serious and common problem for believers and is, at its heart, believing that God is not faithful. This is certainly the problem with grumbling of any kind – at its heart it is saying, 'God is not good; God has not given me what I need.' Believers need to see this as a serious issue and this passage in Numbers helps bring that into focus.

An alternative way in might be to ask about causes of death. For example, in the Napoleonic naval wars (Nelson etc.), what was the biggest killer on board ship? Shipwreck? Battle wounds? The answer is disease. What was the biggest killer in the desert for the Israelites? Was it malnutrition? Battle wounds? Dangerous animals? No, the biggest killer was grumbling. Have you ever grumbled, we could ask our congregation?

Ideas for application

+ Our journey will not be easy and so there will always be a temptation to grumble. We need to be realistic about the dangerous nature of such displeasure.

+ Faith in God's character should lead to contentment – he is both sovereign and caring. Grumbling is always a rejection of God's divine nature.

- Our motivation for life should be the glory of God. Even the practicalities of life should fit within this framework.

- Moses is a great leader, but flawed. As such, he leaves us longing for a greater prophet (Deut. 18:15).

- Christians must learn to be content in Christ remembering God's faithfulness to provide all we need for life and godliness.

Suggestions for preaching

Sermon 1

The passage in 1 Corinthians 10 is a good control for all of these rebellion passages. Paul shows us the danger of following the same path as the wandering Israelites. But he also gives us the encouragement of knowing, like the Israelites, that Christ our Rock is with us. Therefore, though we need to be careful, we need not lose heart. There is a way out of every temptation because God is faithful.

It might be appropriate to let this negative tone direct the preaching. It is right to be sober about sobering passages. However, the sermon can end positively speaking about the forgiveness that Christ offers, the help he gives to those facing temptation, and the desire to be holy (also a strong theme at the end of the Hebrews passage, see Hebrews 4:14-16).

- Don't deny God's goodness (11:4-9; 18-20; 31-35). This point is picking up on the Israelite's wish for food and that it is, at its heart, a denial of the blessings they have received. They deserve and receive judgement. Getting to the heart of their objection is important to make the point relevant today. Christians have received all kinds of richest blessings from our Lord, not least our salvation. However, our focus is very often on what we don't have rather than in rejoicing in what we do.

+ Don't doubt God's power (11:10-17; 21-25). This point addresses Moses' objections and his own grumbling. It is worth pointing out to congregations that grumbling is a disease that spreads. Some Christians think that they can keep their leaders sharp by complaining all the time: "it keeps them on their toes." But in reality, all that happens is that such discontent spreads. Leaders are especially prone to the temptation of believing that God cannot do what he has promised or done in the past. They start believing, like Moses, that it is all about them. It will be important for preachers and teachers to point out that the leadership of Moses does not directly translate to leaders today. Moses points us towards Christ (Heb. 3:2 quotes Num. 12:7). However, there are principles that we can still apply. Unwarranted grumbling against church leaders is sadly commonplace.

+ **Don't disregard God's glory** (11:26-30). This third point refers to Joshua's concern for Moses' glory. No doubt he is well intentioned. But his focus is misplaced and Moses has to rebuke him. We are similarly misguided when we are concerned for the glory of our leaders/church/denomination above that of Christ.

+ **Don't dismiss God's leaders** (12:1-16). Here is a stark warning for all believers. Discontent with leaders is often dressed up in other language (as here, v. 1). And though Moses is a different sort of leader, such dismissal is still a rejection of those the risen and ascended Christ has appointed over us (Eph. 4:11).

The conclusion would need to draw these threads together and use the positive exhortation of 1 Corinthians 10 as outlined above.

Sermon 2

It would be quite possible to focus in on the issue of grumbling and the desires of the Israelites for different (and they think, better) food. Such a message could explore the kinds of things we grumble about and what lies behind our malaise. The danger with such a message is that the grumbling of the people and the disbelief of Moses are intertwined in the passage. Stripping out Moses' sin rather makes a message sound like the preacher is having a go at a congregation and using the sermon to bolster his own position. He could hardly be accused of that if he includes his own temptation to grumble alongside that of his people!

Sermon 3

Another possible message is based on Numbers 12. This would have the advantage of making more of the Lord's endorsement of Moses and drawing lines to Christ like those in Hebrews 3:1-6. Christ was 'faithful to the one who appointed him, just as Moses was faithful in all God's house' (v. 2) and 'Jesus has been found worthy of greater honour than Moses...' The application is clear: 'fix your thoughts on Jesus, the apostle and high priest whom we confess' (v. 1).

Suggestions for teaching

Questions to help understand the passage

1. Read through the passage together and note who is doing the complaining and what they are complaining about.

2. Why do you suppose we get the introductory section in 11:1-3?

3. What is the significance of the people's complaint in verses 4 to 9? What have they forgotten?

4. What is the significance of Moses' complaint in verses 10 to 15? What has he forgotten?

5. Why is Joshua's concern misplaced (11:28-29)?

6. How does God judge the people? Look up Romans 1:24 for a similar example of this kind of judgement.

7. What is at the heart of Miriam's and Aaron's objections? How does God respond?

Questions to help apply the passage

1. What sorts of things do we grumble about? Why? Use the passage to help you think about different areas of church life and personal life.

2. When we are discontent what are we saying about God's character and power?

3. How might we reject those leaders God has placed over us?

4. What does Paul say we should learn from this passage (see 1 Cor. 10:10)?

5. How does Paul say we should live in the light of this passage (see 1 Cor. 10:11-13)?

6. How does being in a church help us fight these battles?

7. Moses was a great leader, but how does the story leave us longing for a better leader, and how do we see that fulfilled in Christ Jesus?

6
REBELLION (13–14)

Introduction

Chapter 13 of Numbers finds the people camped right at the edge of the promised land. This is not only the place from which the scouting party would have set out, but should have been the launch site for the conquest itself. How different things could have been! Numbers could have been a very short book indeed.

However, the grumbling of chapters 11 and 12 has prepared us to expect that things would not be that straightforward, and so it proves to be. These two chapters are important in the Numbers story. They explain why this first generation wandered for forty years then fell in the wilderness. It is this failure that the writer to the Hebrews comments so extensively on. Moreover, they demonstrate the recklessness of not accepting the Lord's punishment: the people disastrously choose to go in to the land anyway after Yahweh has spoken a word of judgement. These two chapters are the clearest indication yet that inheriting the land is no foregone conclusion.[1]

Listening to the text

Context and structure

All the action of this section takes place in, or is reported from, the Desert of Paran (13:3). The story's structure is relatively straightforward:

✦	Instructions to the spies:	13:1-20
✦	Spying out the land:	13:21-25
✦	Reporting back and disagreement over next steps:	13:26-33
✦	The people rebel:	14:1-9
✦	God judges the people and Moses intercedes:	14:10-38
✦	The people ignore God's judgement:	14:39-45

Working through the text

Instructions to the spies: 13:1-20

From the start there is a tension between the role of the spies and the fact that the Lord himself is giving the land (v. 1). This is not ever meant to be an evaluation exercise. The Lord is giving the land; the spies are to gather information (explained further in Moses' instructions in verses 17 to 21).

Just as previously, one man is chosen from each tribe. Notable amongst these are Caleb, who comes from the tribe of Judah and Joshua (his name is changed in verse 16 from Hoshea) who belongs to the tribe of Ephraim. These

---

1   Duguid calls this section, 'snatching defeat from the jaws of victory'.

two are from the largest, most powerful tribe (Judah) and one of the smallest, least significant (the half tribe of Ephraim).

Moses' instructions focus on a number of key questions for those who have never seen the promised land, but only heard about it in handed-down stories from their ancestors.

+ What is the land like? (This question is repeated; it is a key question in an agricultural economy.)

+ Are the people there weak or strong, and how many?

+ What kind of towns do people live in?

+ What is the soil like (which sounds like a further repeat of the first question)?

+ Are there trees?

+ Finally, bring back some fruit!

Moses' repetitions can probably be explained by the excitement that is no doubt felt by all the people: so nearly there! No more manna (or quail!). They can almost see the land, taste it, smell it. Will it be all that was promised?

Spying out the land: 13:21-25
The next section simply describes the extent of the exploration and the successful foraging of some fruit of the land which was in season. However, there are some interesting details:

+ The three Anakite tribes mentioned (Ahiman, Sheshai and Talmai, verse 22) are all driven out by Caleb himself in the later conquest (see Joshua 15:14).

+ Anak means long neck, people who are noted for their height – and this will become a sticking point in the agonising debate that will soon follow.

+ Grapes are a significant fruit throughout the Old Testament, representing fruitfulness, productivity and permanence. It's an unambiguous treasure with which to return.

+ Finally, the last reference to the length of the foray is key to what follows: forty days (v. 25).

Reporting back and disagreement over next steps: 13:26-33
Not surprisingly, everyone awaits their return! But a note of concern is evident in the spies' report. Yes, the land is rich and fertile (literally, 'flow[ing] with milk and honey'). But there are two key problems: 'the people who live there are powerful, and the cities are fortified and very large.' The power of the inhabitants is confirmed by their ancestry.

No doubt the grumbling of chapters 11–12 returns at this point because Caleb has to first silence the people.[2] His response is, sensibly, simply to claim the promises of God already made (not least in verse 1): 'we should go up and take possession of the land, for we can certainly do it' (see, for example, Exodus 3:8).

Most resistance to his faithful assurance comes not, at this stage, from the murmuring people, but from the other spies who have travelled with him. The people are too strong, they claim. 'And they spread among the Israelites a bad report about the land they had explored' (v. 32). The report is not just bad because of the effect it causes (sowing doubt); it is also bad because it is unlikely to be true. 'The

---

2   The word for 'silenced' is onomatopoeic – it sounds like its function: *hasa* (we would say, "hush").

land we explored *devours* those living in it. *All the people we saw there are of great size*' (v. 32)(my italics highlight the preposterous nature of their claims). By devours they probably mean the land is infertile or unstable or unforgiving (or all three), none of which is true.

The Anakites, with their long necks, may have been relatively tall – like the Maasai people of Kenya, perhaps – but it is surely overstating the case to say the spies were like grasshoppers in comparison. Moreover, citing the Nephilim (the only other reference to this people being the sobering account in Genesis 6) is bound to cause alarm.

Perhaps there is a grain of truth in their report, but it is undoubtedly a bad report designed to stir up dissent and trouble. And even if what they claimed *was* true, what of it? Hasn't Yahweh defeated the Egyptian superpower and their military might? A population of slightly tall people hardly seems overwhelming!

At this point it is worth pointing out that the only dissenting voice amongst the spies appears to be Caleb. What of Joshua? Is he to be included with the others in verse 31? Verse 6 of the next chapter makes clear that he should not be included. He simply does not join in the conversation at this time, and it is obvious that his faith belongs with that of Caleb. When the Lord commends the two faithful spies, he does so in the same pattern. First Caleb alone is honoured (14:24); then both escape judgement (14:30).

The people rebel: 14:1-9

The first few verses of chapter 14 are full of language that shows (as does the later judgement) that every member of Israel is affected by this 'bad report'. '*All* the people of the community', '*all* the Israelites', 'the *whole* assembly' (vv. 1-2) (my italics): no one is exempt from this faithlessness.

The preacher must work hard here at communicating the shock of their rejection of God's plan. He has rescued them from Egypt for this very purpose: to bring them into the promised land. Now here they are, *and they reject all that he has done.* "'If only we had died in Egypt! Or in this desert! Why is the Lord bringing us to this land only to let us fall by the sword? Our wives and children will be taken as plunder. Wouldn't it be better for us to go back to Egypt?' And they said to each other, "We should choose a leader and go back to Egypt'" (vv. 2-4).

There is so much we could say about this remarkable statement. For example, choosing their own leader is a rejection of Yahweh who has himself chosen Moses to be theirs. But we must understand, above all, that they are rejecting the salvation God has given them. Worse still, they are attributing evil to Yahweh.

This would be like a Christian saying, "I would be so much better off if I was still an unbeliever." To bring the shock of this home, it would be like a rescued Holocaust survivor saying, "I was better off under Hitler." (I use this kind of illustration advisedly, but it seems apposite to expose just what the Israelites are saying.)

Moses, Aaron, Joshua and Caleb certainly react in a way that shows they know the significance of what is being said. Some commentators say that Moses and Aaron prostrate themselves before the Lord, it just happens to be where the people are (v. 5). More likely, given the context and the words of Joshua and Caleb which follow, this is the action of those who are desperate that the Israelites will recant their ill-judged words.

The two righteous spies repeat, with some expansion, the point that Caleb has already made. Note that they don't try to refute the claims of giants and power; they simply remind the Israelites that if the Lord is with them, they will succeed, 'their protection is gone' (v. 9). On this basis, fear of the inhabitants is quite simply a lack of faith in the promise of God.

God judges the people and Moses intercedes: 14:10-38
The words and actions of the faithful leaders fall on deaf ears. Worse, the Israelites even consider stoning them. Now follows a significant moment which echoes back to Exodus 32 and the incident of the golden calf. There (Exod. 32:9-10) Yahweh threatens to destroy the entire nation in one go and start again with Moses. Here he repeats the same judgement. Their sin is indeed grievous: they have treated him with contempt; they have refused to believe in him.

However, just as in Exodus, Moses intercedes for Israel. And his argument is very similar to that which worked so effectively before. He appeals to Yahweh's fame in the nations (vv. 13-16) and his character, revealed to Moses (vv. 17-19). Pardon them, cries Moses, just as you have before. As an aside, this intercession of Moses contains two great motivations for prayer which preachers might do well to teach their people. This is, perhaps, what it means for the Lord to show himself to be holy ('hallowed by thy name').

We should see, however, that mercy and justice sit together in God's character. He forgives 'sin and rebellion' but there are consequences of sin (v. 18). This is exactly how things play out. The Lord does forgive (v. 20) but this does not mean that things return to how they were and that the people can simply march into the land. No! There is a consequence which is that 'not one of them will ever see the land I promised on oath to their forefathers. No one who has treated me with contempt will ever see it' (v. 23). Only Joshua and Caleb are exempt from this justice.

Rather, the people are to turn back the way they came the very next morning. This judgement is giving the people what they want, even to the extent that they will be travelling *in the direction of Egypt!* 'I will do to you the very things I heard you say' (v. 28). And so, every one of the adults over the age of 20 will die in the desert. Verse 29 is a rather macabre reference back to the census. The census, remember, was counting those who could fight. Now it will serve as a death notice. It is only the children of this generation who will be able to enter into the land. This punishment will not be immediate (otherwise the generations could not be preserved; who, for example, would look after the little ones or nurse the infants?). Rather they will stumble around the wilderness for forty years, 'one year for each of the forty days you explored the land' (v. 34). And this is not going to be a grand adventure like charting a route to the poles. 'You will suffer for your sins and know what it is like to have me against you' (v. 34).

The ten faithless spies do, however, meet an immediate end (vv. 36 and 37) and who can say that this was unjust? The section ends with a further commendation of Joshua and Caleb, just in case any reader had missed it so far.

The passage leaves the question of the Levites unanswered. Were they also included in this judgement? We must assume not because Eleazar the priest, son of Aaron is part of the Joshua generation and almost certainly over 20 years old (his son features as an adult in chapter 25). Eleazar survives to enter the promised land and, as he is not mentioned here, it may well be that the Levites are not included in this comprehensive rebellion. It is quite possible for the text to speak of all Israel and not to include the Levites – they are, after all, not counted with the other tribes.

The people ignore God's judgement: 14:39-45
The last few verses of chapter 14 describe the first battle in Numbers; it does not go well. Perhaps it is possible to sense the frustration that the Israelites feel. They are almost there; they can quite possibly *see* the promised land. So, the next morning, when they should have been turning back south (v. 25) they actually decide to fight anyway.

The irony of this decision is unambiguous. The people were scared to go into the promised land because the opposition was too powerful! Nonsense, said Caleb, if the Lord is with us, we shall be victorious! Now that the Lord has said he will be against them (v. 34) what do they do? They try to conquer. Any careful reader will know how this is going to go. Moses tries to dissuade them (vv. 41 to 43) making just these points.

'Nevertheless, in their presumption, they went up towards the high hill country, though neither Moses nor the ark of the Lord's covenant moved from the camp. Then the Amelekites and Canaanites who lived in that hill country came down and attacked them and beat them down all the way to Hormah' (vv. 44-45).

Hormah means, rather appropriately, 'place of destruction.' And so it is. Sin is not covered by a quick confession. It requires submission to Yahweh's sovereign will, and if the people cannot grasp that now, of all times, how on earth will they fare on their forty year trail? Not well, we expect.

From text to message

Getting the message clear: the theme
Faith is required to inherit the promised land. Faithlessness rejects the promises of God and is worthy of God's severest judgement.

Getting the message clear: the aim

It is this rebellion in particular that the writer to the Hebrews has in mind in chapters 3 and 4. Perhaps, then, we should pick up on his aims and exhortations: 'See to it that none of you has a sinful unbelieving heart' (Heb. 3:12) and 'Let us, therefore, make every effort to enter that rest, so that no one will fall by following their example of disobedience' (Heb. 4:11).

A way in

An introduction to this passage needs to reflect the shock of rejecting God's purposes. This is no minor rebellion nor childish strop. This is wishing away our salvation and refusing to believe the promises God has made or the evidence of his goodness in the past that we have all seen. A suitable hook for a sermon or teaching session needs to reflect the enormity of what is happening in the text.

That is why, when I preached this passage, I used the pejorative Holocaust illustration outlined above. A preacher would have to be careful using such an illustration however. An alternative would be to paint a picture of an imaginary Christian, perhaps nearing death. You normally expect such a man or woman to be increasingly confident in the future hope Christ gives us. But what if that person were to turn to us and say, "I wish I'd never been a Christian! I wish I'd stayed a sinner!" That is the shock of the passage.

A further alternative is to set up the biblical tension between assurance (we *will* inherit our promised land) and the warnings that Scripture gives us about making sure we do not fall away. It would be easy to let this passage frighten us (and perhaps it needs to do that to a certain extent), but it actually stands as a warning, not something to undermine our assurance.

Ideas for application

+ It is easy, amidst the spies' rebellion, to lose sight of the richness of the inheritance God has promised his people – it is indeed a land of abundance. Journeying requires Christians to fix their eyes on this great prize.

+ Taking hold of the inheritance is no easy task, but any obstacles are surmountable with Christ's presence going with the people of God.

+ It is no small thing to reject the inheritance (and the manner in which it should be pursued). Such a rejection is a rejection of Yahweh himself.

+ When the Lord does discipline his people, we must accept his discipline as being right and just and, ultimately, for our good (see Hebrews 12).

+ The intercession of Moses prevents the immediate destruction of the people. We have an even better mediator, 'the man Christ Jesus' (1 Tim. 2:5). He is the one who secures our inheritance and gives us freedom from guilt.

+ Fear is often an indicator that we lack any faith in God's promise-keeping nature.

Suggestions for preaching

Sermon 1

My sermon on this passage took as a text the Hebrews commentary: 'make every effort to enter that rest.' Given that Hebrews looks back to this account to make a positive exhortation, I felt it was warranted to do the same. How, though, do we 'make every effort?'

+ **Believe in God's power.** This is essentially the difference between the ten spies and Joshua and Caleb. The two faithful ones believe God can (and will) give them success. The ten do not. Christians need to believe in God's power, the same power which raised Christ from the dead.

+ **Believe in God's sovereignty.** The Israelites do not simply doubt that God is able to bring them into the land; they also doubt that he knows what he is doing. That much is clear at the beginning of chapter 14. A belief in God's sovereignty can be hard, but it is ultimately a comfort and the only way to enter his rest.

+ **Believe in God's leaders.** If only the people had listened to Joshua and Caleb or, later in the passage, Moses and Aaron. These faithful teachers ought to have been heeded.

+ **Believe in God's discipline.** The final section of the passage shows how dangerous it is not to accept the Lord's discipline. The Bible has much to say about this (not least, Hebrews 12).

+ **Believe in God's mercy.** At the heart of this passage is a wonderful prayer by Moses interceding for the people, a prayer which God both hears and answers. The only hope for the people was an intercessor. We too have an intercessor, the 'mediator of a new Covenant' (Heb. 9:15).

Sermon 2

This is a lot of material, so it could be split over two messages. Alternatively, the preacher could focus in on particular aspects. Moses' intercessory prayer (if set rightly in the context of what is going on) reveals much about intercession and, ultimately, our own great High Priest, Jesus Christ.

The prayer of intercession (14:13-19)

+ Appeals to the glory and renown of our sovereign King (14:13-16)

+ Appeals to the character and nature of our merciful Lord (14:17-19)

Such prayer is answered (14:20)!

Suggestions for teaching

Questions to help understand the passage

1. What task are the spies given (13:17-20)?

2. What do they discover and how do they report it back (13:26-33)? Do you think they are telling the truth?

3. How does Caleb intervene (13:30)?

4. How are the people affected (14:1-4) and how do Moses, Aaron, Joshua and Caleb respond (14:5-9)?

5. What does the Lord declare he will do (14:10-12)? Has this happened before? If so, when?

6. What does Moses base his prayer of intercession on (14:13-19)?

7. How does the Lord respond?

8. If the people are forgiven (14:20) why are there still consequences? What are these consequences (14:21-38)?

9. What should the people be doing the next day (14:25)? What do they do instead (14:39-40)?

10. What is the result and why?

Questions to help apply the passage

1. What is our promised land and what, exactly, has God promised about it?

2. Why should we be certain about getting there?

3. What makes us doubt our final destination?

4. What does the passage teach us about the significance of such doubt?

5. Who intercedes for Christians today?

6. What part do our prayers have as we travel towards our promised land?

7. What does the sin of presumption (14:44) look like today and how do we avoid it?

7
GRACE (15)

Introduction

Considering that the last few chapters have been action-packed and fast-paced, chapter 15 comes as something of an unexpected interruption. (Readers should be grateful for the breather: things carry on as before in chapter 16.) One of the key questions to answer therefore is why does this passage come here, precisely at this point? Why does it not belong with other laws, for example in Leviticus?

Answering that question will unlock the passage and make it possible for the preacher or Bible teacher to teach it faithfully and in line with its original purpose. It seems likely to 'have been placed here as a deliberate comment on the preceding narrative.'[1] The immediate context is that the people of Israel have rejected their salvation from Yahweh.

---

1   Gordon J Wenham, *Numbers: an introduction and commentary* (Nottingham, UK: IVP, 1981), p. 142

They have said they would rather be back in Egypt before the great Rescue. They would rather have their own leader, as opposed to the leader of God's choosing (14:1-4). This rebellion was significant and we have already seen that God's first judgement (before Moses' intercession) would have been to wipe all the people out; in short, they didn't want him and they would get their wish.

Now we can see the purpose of chapter 15 for it shows that the Lord still has an ongoing desire to have a relationship with his people. He still wants to be their God and for them to be his people. Thus the laws address how they may approach him; how forgiveness can be obtained (and what cannot be forgiven); how the people will remember him.

This chapter is thus about *grace*. Some of the most popular sermons on this chapter from the website sermoncentral.com[2] show how often this point is missed; titles like 'Keeping the Sabbath today' and, more absurdly, 'How to use tassels in worship' demonstrate that many readers miss this central truth. More than ever, setting the text in its context is the best way to get behind the precise point of the passage.

It is worth saying a little about laws in general. Christians today are divided about how to understand the Old Testament law; whether to take the Reformers three-fold division (moral, civil and ceremonial) or whether to understand the law in its entirety as pointing to Christ but not having ongoing moral command simply because it is the law. This is not the place to evaluate the options. However, I have assumed that, whatever approach one takes, the

---

2   Accessed 15 November 2011 and a good reason to be wary of such resources!

law – at its very least – points to timeless truths about the relationship between God and his people and, therefore, ultimately takes us to Christ Jesus.

Listening to the text

Context and structure

The NIV heading ('Supplementary offerings', ESV: 'Laws about sacrifices') hardly seems to do justice to a chapter on grace. That is the context in which the laws are repeated here (even if, chronologically, they were not actually *given* at this point). They begin with a clear indication that God still expects the people to enter into the promised land, '*After* you come into the land you are to inhabit…' (v. 2, my italics). The text splits neatly into three component parts, but, for once, the added NIV headings do not help us. The three sections are relatively easy to identify because each begins with the important phrase, 'The Lord said…'

+ Table sacrifices (15:1-16)

+ Dough offering and atonement for sins (15:17-36)

+ Remembering the Lord (15:37-41)

Working through the text

Table sacrifices (15:1-16)

The grace of these rules is both explicit and implicit. It is explicit in verse 2 (repeated in verse 18), 'After you come into the land you are to inhabit…' But it is also implicit throughout the section; we have a picture of abundance in terms of flour, oil and wine. These three are all products of a settled agricultural nation. None of these three can be manufactured or produced on the go whilst in the desert.

The basic premise of this section is that every burnt offering must be accompanied by a food offering (ESV, verse 10, although this is, curiously, a more liberal translation than the NIV which more accurately reflects the text). This food offering is to be a 'grain offering' and a 'drink offering.' These table offerings, as some call them, are something new. Grain offerings as an accompaniment to burnt offerings are mentioned in Leviticus (specifically, Leviticus 8:26-29) but they relate to very specific occasions. Wine offerings are also something altogether new apart from a very brief reference in the laws regarding the Nazirite (see Numbers 6:15).

The novelty of this law seems to be that these food offerings must now accompany every burnt offering. The question is, why is this law introduced at this moment? The best answer seems to be that they are reminders and evidence of grace. The offerings are generous and dependent upon an abundant land. They are also (vv. 11 to 16) extended to all those in the land, including foreigners (NIV, 'aliens'). This is not an admission that the Israelites will be unsuccessful in totally driving out the inhabitants of Canaan (though that will be the case, see Judges 1:21, 27). Rather, it is a recognition early on in the Bible story, that the promise to Abraham (Gen. 12:3) will bring blessing to all nations.

It is important to see that these sacrifices are not atonements for specific sins, but fellowship offerings – the offerings required to maintain fellowship with Yahweh.

Dough offering and atonement for sins (15:17-36)
Although verse 17 seems to continue the same section it actually starts a new one. This is seen by the introductory formula ('The Lord said') and by a change of subject. The theme moves from fellowship offerings (which are about maintaining fellowship with the Lord) to firstfruits offerings

(which serve as reminders). A reader of the Pentateuch is already familiar with this kind of offering: crops (Exod. 23:19 and Leviticus 23:9); animals (Num. 8:17); later, grain and fleece (Deut. 18:4); even first born sons (Num. 8:17-18, though the Levites are consecrated to the Lord in their place).

Once again, it is an offering that can only be given by a conquering people and this point is made both explicitly (v. 18) and implicitly. Baking bread with flour from the threshing floor (v. 20) is something you can only do when you are firmly settled. Baking bread was a regular, if not daily occurrence. Thus, the significance of this offering is of a daily (or at least, six days a week) reminder that the Lord has brought them into the land. No wonder it is to be repeated by future generations (v. 21). Colloquially then, every time an Israelite is kneading the dough he or she should be thinking to himself, 'yes, it's the Lord who has brought me here.' (Whether this law was kept we do not know, but its effect was certainly limited – compare Judges 2:10.)

The next part barely seems to connect; yet it is joined with an important conjunction 'now' (v. 22, esv 'but'). The connection does make sense; it will be hard for a Hebrew to remember being brought into the land without reflecting on the inglorious way the nation behaved. Sin needs remedy. Various scenarios are envisaged:

+ Unintentional community sin (involving all the people) (15:22-26)

+ Unintentional personal sin (involving one person) (15:27-29)

+ Defiant personal sin (15:30-36)

Before getting to the detail of the text, it is important for the preacher/teacher to understand (and explain) the difference between unintentional sin and defiant sin. Unintentional sin seems relatively straightforward; it is sin that is committed without malice or deliberate action. On this basis, an example of an unintentional sin might be offending someone with words when there was no intention to cause offence.

The trouble with this definition is two-fold. Firstly, sin is rarely completely devoid of motive even if (in the case above), the fault is one of omission – failing to think carefully enough about the effect one's words might have on a fellow believer. The second problem is that this chapter follows on directly from chapter 14 where we have encountered a corporate rebellion of the most severe kind but which *is* forgiven (see 14:20) by Yahweh. It is hardly, on the definition above, unintentional.

Perhaps, then, it is best to define unintentional as the opposite of defiant which is helpfully illustrated with a worked example (15:32-36)[3] and the disastrous consequences of the rebellion in chapter 16. The ESV helpfully translates 'defiantly' as 'with a high hand.' This kind of sin is raising a closed fist to God. It is not, therefore, 'falling into sin' or being 'overcome with sin' – it is a deliberate embracing of sin in defiance against the Lord.

---

3   Duguid uses the illustration of manslaughter (where an imprudent action leads to someone's death) and murder (where there is an intention to kill) to show the difference. But I wonder if that illustration is not quite sufficient? The defiance of verses 30 to 31 and the subsequent punishment seems to be something even more than adding premeditation to sinful action, which seems to be forgiven, for example when it comes to David and Bathsheba (2 Sam. 11–12) or even the rebellion in chapter 14. Chapters 16 and 17 seem to further illustrate defiant sin. Duguid, p. 190

Its parallel in the New Testament is almost certainly the unforgiveable sin of Mark 3:20-30 which attributes evil to God and consequently leads to rebellion against him.[4] As with all such passages, preachers and teachers should be aware of listeners or participants who are particularly sensitive and will worry that they have committed sin that is unforgiveable. Someone who is anxious about such things demonstrates by their concern that their sin *is* pardonable. On this basis unintentional sin is best defined as sin that is *not* defiant: the two categories are "defiant" and "not defiant."

It is interesting that corporate sin (vv. 22 to 26) is thus dealt with before individual sin (vv. 27-29). This reflects the corporate nature of the relationship with Yahweh that the people have; indeed, this unity has been a common theme throughout Numbers so far. Such sins are forgivable if appropriate atonement is made. What is true corporately is also true individually. As with the earlier regulations of this chapter, the individual laws are also extended to aliens living in the land.

A key theme here is that atonement is required for sin to be forgiven. The Lord cannot simply forgive and forget. A price is required and 'without the shedding of blood there is no forgiveness' (Heb. 9:22 paraphrasing Leviticus 17:11). Grace is neither free nor cheap. It is costly, ultimately costing the death of the Son of God himself. The danger of a redeemed people on their way to the promised land is always that salvation will be taken for granted. The sacrificial system, at its very least, demonstrated that forgiveness was no small matter. Given all that we have seen in the recent chapters of Numbers, how ever will Israel survive and

---

4   This is helpfully explained by James Philip, *Numbers, the Preachers Commentary Series vol. 4* (Nashville, USA: Thomas Nelson, 1987), p. 168

inherit the promised land unless there is atonement and forgiveness?

There are, however, sins that cannot be forgiven. These are the defiant sins which are, in effect, 'blasphemy against the Lord' (i.e. breaking the third commandment). Such a sinner must be thrown out of the nation ('cut off from his people') and his guilt cannot be removed by sacrifice, it 'remains on him' (v. 31). What such sin might be and how such a sinner might be 'cut off' is now explained in a little worked example. Whether this incident took place at this point in the chronology of Numbers is neither here nor there. Its relevance here is as an illustration of the kind of defiance the chapter describes.

At first the man's sin seems harmless enough: gathering wood on a Sabbath (v. 32). But this is a significant sin. It is, in fact, a double transgression of the fourth commandment. Not only is he doing the work of gathering wood on the Sabbath, but he is (we presume) going to light a fire. What else might the wood be for? Lighting a fire on the Sabbath was also prohibited (see Exodus 35:3) and some commentators have helpfully pointed out that such an act is defiant in itself. Everyone sees a fire! The man is effectively parading his disobedience and saying that Yahweh's good laws are of no matter to him whatsoever. His defiance is, in effect, thumbing his nose at the Lord.

The rules of verses 30 and 31 must therefore be applied and thus he receives the death sentence which is duly carried out (the obedience refrain of verse 36 implies that this story perhaps belongs chronologically with the earlier chapters of Numbers). The man's defiance sets us up for the rebellions of the next few chapters.

Remembering the Lord (15:37-41)

The Sabbath-breaker's story would be a rather sober end to a chapter on grace and thankfully there is a little more. The section about tassels (vv. 37-41) seems a little obscure until we realise that they are designed to serve a very important purpose, 'you will remember to obey all my commands and will be consecrated to your God. I am the Lord your God who brought you out of Egypt to be your God. I am the Lord your God' (vv. 40-41).

Here is a repetition of the salvation formula (see also 1:1) but with an added ingredient; the reason the Lord has saved the people is so that they can *be* his people. Suddenly the laws of this chapter make sense. Yahweh must provide for continuing fellowship with Israel (hence the offerings) and also for when things do go wrong (atonement). But there must also be cleansing and purification of those who do not want Yahweh to be their God, hence the rules concerning defiant sin.

Moreover, the people must take care to remember the Lord and all that he has done and commanded. They need a regular reminder not to follow the 'lusts of [their] own hearts and eyes' (v. 39). This is the function of the tassels. They are blue (also the colour of the tabernacle) and are fitted to all the clothes the Israelites wear. Whenever they get dressed or do the washing or see one another in the street, they should remember the Lord.

From text to message

Getting the message clear: the theme

It is crystal clear the Lord wants to continue in relationship with his people. He has saved them and he wants them to enter into the promised land and for him to be their God and they his people. They will need his grace for this to happen which he willingly and abundantly gives.

Getting the message clear: the aim
We also need the grace of Christ not just to be saved but to go on with Christ. Though forgiven sinners, our hearts are not perfect yet and we need to go on remembering and relying on the once-for-all sacrifice of the Lord Jesus for us.

A way in
It is not easy to introduce such a passage and hook people into its message of grace. It might be useful for the preacher or teacher to remind people that things have almost come to an end for Israel (14:11-12). It hardly looks promising. Unless there is some work of grace on God's part it is highly unlikely that the Israelites will ever get to Canaan.

An alternative would be to address questions that people might be asking after hearing the passage being read. Numbers 15 is not about cooking, baking, embroidery or whether we watch television on a Sunday. It is about relationship with the living God and the only way that we can have a relationship with God – by grace.

A more contemporary illustration might be the defiance shown by the US sprinters Tommie Smith and John Carlos at the 1968 Mexico Olympics. They notoriously raised their fists on the medal rostrum in a gesture of defiance against oppression back home saying, in effect, 'you don't rule over me; I'm not yours.' They were stripped of their titles and medals for deliberately breaking the rules against making political statements at sporting events (even though the political point they were making was valid). Sinning against God is both serious and something from which we all suffer. Can we really keep going with the Lord with such rebellious hearts?

Ideas for application

+ God gives a sacrifice that will enable his people to maintain a relationship with him. It has a once-to-many nature reminding us of the once-for-all sacrifice of Christ Jesus.

+ God also gives means of grace to his people to enable them to remember what he has done – primarily for Christians this is the Lord's Supper.

+ The passage is also realistic about the ongoing nature of sin and the need for constant mediation. Our perfect High Priest intercedes for us as we journey with him. His intercession means we can continue to enjoy the benefits of his once-for-all sacrifice.

Suggestions for preaching

This passage is best taken as one section because the theme of grace pervades it all and splitting it up would lose the overall thrust which is that we can walk with Christ to our promised destination because of grace. But what is grace? We would do well to follow the text's own divisions:

+ **God does not treat us as our sins deserve** (vv. 1-16). Although Numbers seems, at times, very bloodthirsty, the real surprise is that it is not more so. God would be quite within his rights to have destroyed Israel at least three times over already! But here is a provision for people to continue in relationship with him, settled in the promised land. This is grace.

+ **God forgives the sinner who repents** (vv. 17-36). Though this section does contain the difficult section about defiant sins, the overall thrust is that God will forgive and bring people home to their inheritance. Perhaps the section on defiance could be considered separately, but to do so would be to lose the theme of the passage which majors on grace and forgiveness. [A fourth point, for example, might be **God's patience is not inexhaustible** (Num. 15:30-36)]. Nevertheless, as we have seen above, some careful explanation of this section will be required. Continued forgiveness is grace.

+ **God reminds us of our walk with him** (vv. 37-41). The tassels are not for today. What the Old Covenant externalised is now internalised. We have the inward witness of the Spirit to tell us we are God's children (Rom. 8:16). However, New Testament believers also have a physical means of grace and remembrance in the Lord's Supper which is given precisely so that we do not forget (1 Cor. 11:24-25).

Suggestions for teaching

Questions to help understand the passage

1. What evidence is there that (despite the previous rebellions) the Israelites will eventually make it to the promised land? (See, especially vv. 1 and 17).

2. What purpose do these offerings serve (vv. 7, 10 and 14)?

3. Who should bring them (vv. 15 and 16) and why does this remind the people of the covenant with Abraham (Gen. 12)?

4. What is the point of a firstfruits offering like that described in verses 17 to 21?

5. Verses 22-31 describe three different types of sin. What are they?

6. Which can be forgiven and which cannot? Why?

7. What is an example of a forgivable sin? Use the stories you have read so far in Numbers to help you.

8. Numbers 14:32-36 describes a defiant sin. Why is this particular sin so serious?

9. What purpose do the tassels described in verses 37-41 serve?

Questions to help apply the passage

1. How does the passage's certainty about the Israelites' inheritance give us confidence in our own?

2. Why are offerings no longer required to receive forgiveness from God?

3. Why are offerings no longer required to maintain fellowship with God?

4. How might a church (as a people) sin against God?

5. What is the New Testament equivalent of defiant sin? Read Mark 3:20-30 for help.

6. How, as Christians, can we remember what God has done for us in Christ?

8
REJECTION (16–18)

Introduction

Chapters 16 through to 18 take us back to familiar territory. The moment of grace held out by chapter 15 turns out to be a very brief oasis in a desert (literally) of rebellion. Up to now, the children of Israel have rejected Yahweh (and, specifically, his sovereign purposes) and Moses, their God-appointed leader. Now the focus shifts slightly to repeat those similar themes, but also to include Aaron the priest. Like a previous rebellion section (chs. 11 and 12) this section has two complaints intertwined together. At first Korah, Dathan and Abiram are all grouped together. However, they come from different tribes and present with slightly different issues.

+ Korah, a Levite, thinks that the priestly provisions are too restrictive, that other members of the nation are also holy and, more specifically, that fellow Levites should be allowed to 'get the priesthood.'

◆ Dathan and Abiram (Reubenites) have more general objections and refuse to submit to Moses' leadership (vv. 12-14).

All three (and their families) are judged together. But this is not the end of the story. The judgement stirs up the same old rebellion in the people once more – this time expressed in a rejection of Moses' and Aaron's leadership. Once again, Yawheh's righteous fury is total, but atonement is made and the Lord's anger subsides.

Chapter 17 reinforces (through supernatural means) the choosing of Aaron as priest. Chapter 18 sits neatly with it as a reinforcement of earlier chapters regarding the place of the Levites; it adds, however, one new piece of information about their role in protecting the people from the wrath of God, an addition which is highly relevant given the narrative that has preceded it.

This section might, at first glance, appear to add nothing new to the rebellion story. However, it introduces the idea of rejection of the priesthood alongside the rejection of both Yahweh and his servant Moses. Yahweh's anger is still kindled. In fact, the passage now accentuates that he *cannot* be approached, except on his own terms.

There is also significance in the fact that this is another nationwide rebellion. The people have not learnt their lesson. Their hearts are still turned away from God and their actions reveal it for us to see, making sure we don't repeat their mistakes.

Moreover, though we have seen atonement in action already in Numbers, here in chapter 16 its purpose becomes very clear as it turns away the wrath of God and prevents judgement from overtaking the people. In summary we could say that this section takes familiar themes and multiplies them.

Listening to the text

Context and structure

The story has a number of acts and scenes, much like a theatre play or movie:

Act 1: Korah, Dathan and Abiram's rebellion

- ✦ Rebellion (16:1-15)
- ✦ God's judgement (16:16-21)
- ✦ Intercession (16:22-27)
- ✦ God's judgement (16:28-35)
- ✦ Reminder (censers) (16:36-40)

Act 2: The nation's rebellion

- ✦ Rebellion (16:41)
- ✦ God's judgement (16:42-45)
- ✦ Intercession (atonement) (16:46-48)
- ✦ God's judgement (16:49-50)
- ✦ Reminder (Aaron's staff) (17:1-12)

Act 3

- ✦ Reminder (role of Levites and priests) (18:1-32)

There is a clear pattern in the first two acts of rebellion-judgement-atonement (or intercession)-reminder. On this reading chapter 18 seems less connected as it does not follow the same pattern and it could easily form a separate sermon.

Working through the text

Act 1: Korah, Dathan and Abiram's rebellion

Rebellion (16:1-15)

The passage begins with a curious collection of rebels. Korah seems to be chief amongst them here (the rebels are later called 'his followers', see verse 19). Korah is a Kohathite, of the same Levite clan as Moses and Aaron. His co-conspirators are three Reubenites: Dathan, Abiram and On. The first two are also identiftied as ring leaders in Psalm 106:16-18. On is not mentioned again; possibly because he thinks better of it. With them are 250 other senior Israelite men. We must assume that these included men from all different tribes as this makes best sense of the action in chapter 17 and explains why Zelophehad's daughters are at pains to point out that their father was not in this rebel group (see 27:3). Zelophehad was from the tribe of Manasseh.

There is just a hint that this rebellion is deeper than the grumblings of a few people as the 250 are 'chosen from the assembly' (v. 2, ESV). Their complaint (v. 3) seems to be a priestly one, but there may be other grumblings going on. From Moses' reaction, addressed in particular to Korah (vv. 4-11) there seems to be a primary issue of whether there is a difference between Levites and priests. The response of Dathan and Abiram seems to introduce a slightly different complaint (vv. 12-14). It seems to be less an issue of priesthood and more one of authority or leadership.

However, each one is tested in the same way, with a censer (a priestly function). Therefore perhaps it is best to see the complaints from all the 250 as being roughly equal ('why should Aaron be the priest?') but that when Moses tackles it he deals with Levites and non-Levites separately. He could hardly appeal to non-Levites with the words he addresses to Korah.

We have seen Moses' reaction before ('he fell facedown', verse 4). Once again, this is a serious rebellion because it is Yawheh himself who has appointed Aaron and his sons. Thus rejecting Aaron is the same as rejecting the Lord. Moses knows this so he sets up a trial by censer – a very appropriate test to show 'who belongs to [the Lord] and who is holy and he will have that person come near to him' (v. 5).

Levites should know better, says Moses! They have a high calling, separated (but not made holy, see notes on 8:5-22). They are nearer the tabernacle than any other tribe. Why do they want the priesthood too? Moses sees clearly the significance of their grumbling: 'It is against the Lord that you and all your followers have banded together' (v. 11). It is Yahweh who calls men into priesthood. The writer to the Hebrews almost certainly has this point in mind when he examines the priesthood of Jesus: 'no one takes this honour upon himself – he must be called by God, just as Aaron was' (Heb. 5:4).

Moses also wants words with the two other conspirators. But they are unwilling to come because they do not recognise Moses' leadership (this is more than a childish strop). His leadership is misguided and he has not delivered on his promises (vv. 12-14), they claim. Their little response speech is bookended by the simple rejection, 'we will not come.' They cannot see the irony of their position in the wilderness which is that the lack of progress is not down to Moses' leadership but the very complaints against Yahweh like the ones they are making here! Note that Dathan and Abiram actually identify

Egypt as the land flowing with milk and honey, rather like a Christian saying he liked the sound of hell!

God's judgement (16:16-21)

However much common ground (or not) there is between these two groups, they are treated in the same way when it comes to judgement. Moses shares Yahweh's righteous indignation (v. 15). There follows a test by censer, at this stage a procedure that seems to have been initiated by Moses. The censer is a key part of the priest's armoury (see, for example, Leviticus 16:12) and all the participants willingly agree. Stupidly, they assume that their case will be vindicated by Yawheh.

Verses 20 and 21 are not straightforward. Who gathers?; to whom does the Lord appear?; against whom is his anger directed? These are questions that all turn on the word *eda* (translated congregation or assembly). Korah gathers all 'his followers' (*eda*, verse 19) and 'the glory of the Lord appeared to the entire assembly' (*eda*). 'The Lord said to Moses and Aaron, "Separate yourselves from this assembly [*eda*] so I can put an end to them at once"' (vv. 20-21).

The NIV seems to have got the sense right. It is Korah and his followers (*eda*) who gather, watched by the entire nation (*eda*). God's wrath is then directed at the nation (not just Korah's followers) – Moses' plea in verse 22 makes this clear. This is probably because they have been complicit in the rebellion (see verse 2, ESV). Everyone (*eda* again, verse 24) is directed to move away from Korah, Dathan and Abiram who are judged, along with the 250 who also receive due punishment (v. 35). This is not the only time in this section that the entire nation will be on the wrong end of God's wrath; the pattern is repeated in verse 45.

Intercession (16:22-27)

Moses now intercedes for the people, just as he has in the past. Now, though, his argument is that it is wrong for God's wrath to envelop the whole nation when only one man has sinned (v. 22). This seems to be hyperbole on the part of Moses. He knows, at the very least, that Dathan, Abiram and 250 others are equally culpable. Nor should we think that Yahweh has made a mistake in his original judgement, a bit like an angry father might lash out at innocent children.

Rather, Moses' appeal recognises that there are different orders of rebellion here. Korah is the ringleader and his other followers are complicit. But their rebellion must be of an altogether different scale than that of the people who chose them in the first place. As before, the Lord hears Moses and gives instruction for Korah, Dathan and Abiram to be quarantined. Moses repeats the instruction (vv. 25 to 26) and the people comply (v. 27).

There are one or two textual difficulties in this section. First, Moses addresses Yahweh with an extremely unusual title in verse 22, 'God of the spirits of all mankind.' In the Bible it is found only here and in Numbers 27:16 (Moses' prayer for a new leader). It is, apparently, common in post-biblical literature. Some commentators therefore assume it is a later insertion, but there is no reason to think that Moses could *not* have used it. Here it ties in nicely with his appeal on behalf of the whole assembly, God is *their* God.

The second difficulty is that the word for tents (or dwelling, ESV) in verse 24 is singular. It rather implies that the Levite Korah was living in the same area as the Reubenites, Dathan and Abiram. Although at first puzzling, a reminder of the camp layout (ch. 2) will show that the Kohathites are camped to the south, the same side as the Reubenites; their camps adjoin one another. It is not beyond belief to think that this may be precisely how the rebellion took shape – neighbours grumbling and complaining to one another over the 'garden fence.'

God's judgement (16:28-35)

Moses introduces God's judgement by telling the people that the sign of God's approval of Moses will be whether these men die an unnatural death or not. 'But if the Lord brings about something totally new, and the earth opens its mouth and swallows them, with everything that belongs to them, and they go down alive into the grave, then you will know that these men have treated the Lord with contempt' (v. 30). The Lord *does* do something completely new and Korah, Dathan and Abiram, their families and all their possessions are completely devoured. No wonder the Israelites jump away from the site (v. 34). A slightly less unusual punishment awaits those others who have offered unauthorised fire (to use the language of Leviticus 10:1).[1]

A problem for the preacher at this juncture is that the punishment seems to be rather unjustly extended to the families, children and 'little ones' of the rebels. Surely such wrath contradicts the law? 'Fathers shall not be put to death for their children, nor children put to death for their fathers; each is to die for his own sin' (Deut. 24:16). In mitigation we have to say that none of the entire assembly is innocent (v. 21) and that Moses' intercession has been enough to assuage the wrath of God against most but not all of the Israelites.

---

1   Perhaps this is a good illustration of sinning with a high hand (15:30)? Dathan and Abiram are calling what is good, evil and what is evil, good.

However, Numbers 26:11 holds out some hope that some, at least, were saved, perhaps by moving away at Moses' request. Although we know that the rebels' *households* (v. 32) were destroyed, we can't be exactly sure what this means. The second census records that 'the line of Korah, however, did not die out.' Some, at least, were spared.

Reminder (censers) (16:36-40)

This first act is brought to a completion with the Lord's command to Moses to make censers into a covering for the ark where it will serve as a reminder to the people that 'no one except a descendant of Aaron should come to burn incense before the Lord, or he would become like Korah and his followers' (v. 40).

It is Eleazar, Aaron's son, who is to undertake this task. Eleazar will feature heavily in the Numbers story in later chapters. For now, it seems wholly appropriate for someone from the next generation to make this reminder which itself is to serve future generations. Eleazar is one of the descendants of which verse 40 speaks.

Act 2: The nation's rebellion

Rebellion (16:41)

It should come as no surprise that this is not the end of the matter. The 250 who have incurred God's wrath are, at the very least, 'well-known community leaders' (v. 2, NIV) and possibly 'chosen from the assembly' (v. 2, ESV), a sort of democratic council. Their abrupt and dramatic end has not just frightened the Israelites (v. 34) but angered them too. There is lots of this kind of dark irony in Numbers. The 250 wanted the right to burn incense and now they have been burnt themselves! The 'whole Israelite community' rather than rejoicing in Yahweh's provision of Aaron to 'come near' now accuses Moses and Aaron of killing their favourites. Whatever else has happened, however, it's very difficult to see 'something totally new' (v. 30) as being of Moses' doing. Their anger may be vented against Moses and Aaron but it is actually against God.

God's judgement (16:42-45)

So then, this is just the same old grumbling, complaining and rejecting of Yahweh. No wonder the glory of the Lord appears (v. 42). The Lord now instructs Moses to do exactly what he did earlier and then later calls Moses to instruct the people, 'get away from this assembly so I can put an end to them at once' (v. 45, compare verses 21 and 24).

Intercession (atonement) (16:46-48)

Unlike other patterns of rebellion, this time there is no intercession. However, Moses understands that the Lord's wrath is righteous and the danger is real so he instructs Aaron to make atonement. This he does by taking his own (approved) censer, offering incense with 'fire from the altar' (v. 46) and rushing into the assembly. Quite how offering incense from this vantage point makes atonement is not spelt out. Atonement is normally made with the blood of an animal, without which, as we have already seen, there is no forgiveness. It is likely that the fire from the altar represents a sacrifice already made there. Aaron's act is to take the atoning fire and bring it physically into the camp.

God's judgement (16:49-50)

Moses' plan is effective in stopping the plague which has been God's chosen method of judgement this time (v. 48). However, he is not quite in time to prevent the deaths of just under fifteen thousand of the people.

Reminder (Aaron's staff) (17:1-12)

Chapter 17 appears, at first glance, to be an ancillary story. However, the two rebellions follow the same pattern and thus we would expect to see a reminder instituted to ensure that the people do not repeat the mistake of chapter 16 (and in the Hebrew Scriptures this is all counted as part of the same chapter which begins at 16:36). This is the purpose of chapter 17 in which the Lord confirms Aaron as his chosen line for the priesthood. This is not for Moses' nor Aaron's benefit, but for the people's, specifically to arrest their grumbling, 'I will rid myself of this constant grumbling against you by the Israelites' (v. 5).

The Lord's plan is straightforward. Each tribe is to submit a leader's staff, writing the leader's name upon it. Twelve staffs are required, though this number appears to include Levi (v. 3). It would seem strange that the two half-tribes of Ephraim and Manasseh are counted together here, as they are combined nowhere else in Numbers. Most likely, it should be taken as read that Levi's staff is an additional one (and that may be the sense of verse 6). Aaron's name is to be inscribed as the leader of Levi – though this is an unusual title for him. Nowhere else is he described in this way. The plan will have a dual effect; not only will it confirm the uniqueness of Levi amongst the tribes (thereby addressing Dathan and Abiram's complaint), but it will reassert Aaron as chief among the Levites and therefore the rightful recipient of the priestly line. All the staffs are placed before the Lord in the Tent of the Testimony (this is not a new name in Numbers, see 1:50, 9:15, 10:11). The staff that sprouts (v. 5) belongs to the tribe of God's choosing.

It's no surprise that the next day this is Aaron's staff. But in a miracle of abundance, the staff has not just sprouted (producing little shoots perhaps), but has 'budded, blossomed and produced almonds' (v. 8). What a miracle! When Moses brings out the staffs no hunting or close inspection is required. Everyone can clearly see whom God has chosen.

Verses 10 and 11 capture the ongoing significance of this staff. It is to be a reminder (and Hebrews 9:4 records that it was placed *inside* the ark). Wonderfully, the Lord provides this testimony so that the people will stop grumbling 'so that they will not die' (v. 10). Yahweh doesn't *want* his people to die. His very character is loving and gracious, as Moses well knows (Exod. 34:6-7). Yet he is holy and he must be approached his way; the staff will serve as a reminder of this fact.

In an unusually perceptive moment, the people grasp what is being said. It is impossible for them to approach the presence of the Lord as represented in the tabernacle (v. 13). However, true to form, they have misunderstood the significance of what God has already done to prevent them being consumed. They see the case as hopeless 'We will die! We are lost, we are all lost!' (v. 12) but Yahweh has already guarded his holy presence through the provision of the Levites (8:19). The people need to be reminded of this role once again.

Act 3

Reminder (role of Levites and priests) (18:1-32)
Act 3 (ch. 18) then, reminds the people of the roles of the Levites and priests with specific reference to the genuine issue the people have just raised: how will they be protected from the holy and consuming presence of the Lord? In some ways, this chapter contains little new information, but there

is an emphasis we have not previously seen on the guarding role the Levites and priests are to have.

The NIV translation is slightly weak here. The ESV is more helpful representing the work as 'keep guard' (vv. 3, 4, 5 and 7) rather than the more vague NIV 'be responsible.' In the context of 17:12-13, guard duty is an appropriate phrase. This section is not just about sweeping up in the tabernacle but being a Yahweh-sanctioned human shield so that the people do not come too near.

The section is introduced by establishing the Kohathites ('you, your sons and your father's family' – verse 1) as those who will be responsible for ensuring the assembly do not get too near. The choice of the Kohathites seems reasonable as they are the ones who are allowed to get close to the holy things at camp packing time. But who will protect the Kohathites? Aaron and his sons (the priests) take on this task.

However, all the Levites (vv. 2-7) are to share the responsibility for actual guard duty. 'No one else may come near where you are' (v. 4). This will prevent the wrath of the Lord coming on the assembly again. The Levites are given for this task, but just in case there is any doubt, Yahweh reiterates that the priests may only come from Aaron's line (v. 7).

The clarification of the Levites' and priests' duties raises questions about how they are to be funded and provided for. The remainder of chapter 18 deals with this question. Two sections deal with what Aaron (and by implication the line of priests) are to receive (18:8-20) and what the other Levites are to receive (18:21-32). Broadly speaking, the priests are provided for out of the part of the offerings brought whilst the Levites are provided for from the tithes of the nation.

This provision is 'an everlasting covenant of salt' – a difficult phrase which occurs again when the Lord makes a covenant with David (2 Chron. 13:5). It probably refers to the eternal nature of the covenant. Why do the priests need such provision? Quite simply because they will inherit no land (v. 20). Serving the Lord is their 'share and inheritance.'

Likewise the Levites receive no inheritance (v. 24) but are provided for. The idea of a tenth works nicely mathematically. This one tribe is to be supported by eleven others (ten tribes and two half tribes). Roughly speaking, if each tribe brings a tenth then the Levites will enjoy what everyone else enjoys – no more, no less. The tenth is reduced slightly by the Levites offering a tenth of the tenth to the Lord (v. 26), but this is allowed for in the eleven tribes contributing a tenth each. Aaron (and presumably his priestly line) receive this tenth of a tenth.

From text to message

Getting the message clear: the theme

This long section is essentially about the people rejecting Yahweh's own instructions about how they can come near. The consequences are fatal. He is holy and consuming and a sinful people can only approach him on his terms.

Getting the message clear: the aim

God has not changed. His holiness still means that 'our God is a consuming fire' (Heb. 12:29 quoting Deuteronomy 4:24). However, in Christ we can come near because of the atoning work that he has done. We no longer need protection from the presence of God when we are in Christ.

A way in

C.S. Lewis' description of Aslan may be a good place to start a sermon on this passage. God is not 'safe.' He is a lion! But he is good.[2] So though his holy presence is consuming, he has provided a way that he can be known and we can approach him. This section of Numbers sets up the priestly work of Christ on the cross.

Ideas for application

+ Atonement and intercession are effective in stopping and minimising the judgement of God.

+ However, the ongoing capacity of the human heart for rebellion stands in stark contrast to God's mercy.

+ Access to Yahweh is through the priest whom God appoints, not through those who set themselves up as priests – a point the writer to the Hebrews is keen to make (Heb. 5).

+ God continues to provide for his people to be his people and for him to be their God – covenant relationship is always in view. Christians need this ongoing ministry as they journey towards their promised land.

Suggestions for preaching

This is a long section and there may just be too much material to do justice to in one sermon. However, the section does have a unity which could easily be lost in breaking it up.

Sermon 1

To do best justice to the text, the preacher needs to focus on how the people can come to God and how this is ultimately made possible in Christ.

---

2   'Safe?' said Mr Beaver; 'don't you hear what Mrs Beaver tells you? Who said anything about safe 'cause he isn't safe. But he's good. He's the King, I tell you.' Ref – C.S Lewis, *The Lion, The Witch and the Wardrobe* (London, UK, Harper Collins, 2005).

+ **The risk we run when we approach God on our own terms.** It is not difficult to see that approaching God in a way other than that which he has ordained means death. The text makes this clear in the most dramatic way possible. In a world which thinks of God only in terms of kindness and compassion, we also need to be faithful in presenting him as holy and pure. To be casual about him, or to think we can know him when we set the agenda is foolhardy and deathly dangerous.

+ **The access we enjoy when we approach God on his terms.** It is remarkable that God's character is both purity and grace. He does want us to be his people and he provides a way for that to happen. The text reinforces this access, though we have to say it is limited and the people still require protection. Amazingly, the coming of the Lord Jesus as our great High Priest opens access to the Most Holy Place. (It is possible to read chapter 19 as being superfluous in the new covenant in respect to its detail though, of course, not in terms of the one to whom it points).[3]

Sermon 2

Alternatively, Raymond Brown has an outline which he spread over two chapters in his book and in which he focuses in on leadership.[4]

---

3   Although it may well contain useful lessons about providing for ministers, its primary role as an instruction for priests comes to an end with the coming of Christ and the preacher should reflect this in his teaching.

4   Raymond Brown, *The message of Numbers* (Nottingham, UK: IVP Books, 2002), p. 151

- ✦ God's appointed leadership challenged (16:1-14)

- ✦ God's appointed leadership tested (16:15-22)

- ✦ God's appointed leadership vindicated (16:23-50)

- ✦ God's appointed leadership confirmed (17:1–18:7)

- ✦ God's appointed leadership supported (18:8-32)

Such an outline is faithfully descriptive of the text but perhaps does not make enough of the challenge to the *priesthood* of Aaron; this is more than a leadership issue, it is about how people might draw near to the living God.

Suggestions for teaching

Questions to help understand the passage

1. Who are the rebels and what is their grievance? (You will need to read through 16:1-14 to answer this question.)

2. Why is the grumbling of the Levites particularly obnoxious (16:8-10)?

3. What does their complaint boil down to (16:10-11)? Why is this, ultimately, a rejection of the Lord?

4. Why do you suppose the Lord's anger burns against the entire community (16:21)?

5. What happens to the three ringleaders and their families (16:31-33)? What happens to the other complaining leaders (16:35)? Is it deserved?

6. What instruction is Eleazar given? Why?

7. How should the Israelites have responded to this judgement? How do they respond (16:41)?

8. How do Moses and Aaron halt the Lord's judgement?

9. Why is chapter 17 necessary in this story?

10. How do the people respond to the budding of Aaron's staff (17:12-13) and how does this set up the next chapter's explanation?

Questions to help apply the passage

1. What does this passage teach us about God, his character and how we draw near to him?

2. What are some of the ways we might try to approach God on our own terms, rather than his?

3. What, this side of the cross, are God's own terms (see Hebrews 10:12-14)?

4. How does Christ and his work change the requirements of chapter 18?

9
CLEANSING (19)

Introduction

The death toll has been steadily rising. In the last rebellion alone, over fifteen thousand people died. That is a lot of dead bodies in the desert and, as a result, a lot of ceremonial uncleanness amongst God's people. There is little escape in a camp. Just as recent stories from refugee camps have shown how disease can easily spread amongst dense populations, so many Israelites would have contact with a dead body in the camp – and the righteous judgements of God have made the problem more pressing. Ceremonial uncleanness is a serious issue because it placed people outside of the camp and therefore outside of fellowship with Yahweh.

Chapter 19 therefore introduces an innovation to ensure that uncleanness caused by dead bodies can be quickly and effectively addressed without diminishing the significance of death itself. The red heifer should make us think, once again, of the priestly work of Christ to make the unclean clean. Misguided attempts to breed and reintroduce such heifers to modern day Israel rather miss the point of this important pointer to Jesus.[1]

Listening to the text

Context and structure

Chapter 19 follows on logically from the rebellions and judgements that began in chapter 11 and, with a small break, run through to the end of chapter 18. It contains Yahweh's provision for dealing with ceremonial uncleanness in a kind of portable cleansing operation based on water made with ashes from a red heifer.

+ Instructions for making the cleansing water (19:1-10)

+ Instructions for using the cleansing water (19:11-22)

Working through the text

Instructions for making the cleansing water (19:1-10)
Moses and Aaron receive instruction from the Lord to deal with the problem of contact with dead bodies. The perfect red heifer[2] (v. 2) is to be slaughtered outside the camp (where the problem exists – see 5:1-3). Eleazar is to do this work; he may have been chosen because he represents the next generation and this provision is to be a lasting ordinance for Israel (see verses 10 and 21), though most commentators suppose that the high priest Aaron could not go outside the camp. Though the ritual slaughter takes place outside

---

1   See, for example, the news item at http://to.pbs.org/pt1Zh (accessed 17 January 2012)

2   The NIV has followed the LXX translation here, itself picked up in Hebrews 9:13. However, individual purification offerings were often female (e.g. Leviticus 14:10) and the Hebrew word clearly refers to a cow in 1 Samuel 6:7. It may be either male or female.

the camp, it is done with a nod to the atoning work that happens inside the tabernacle – hence the instruction to Eleazar to face the Tent of Meeting as he sprinkles the blood (v. 4), the sprinkling being standard procedure for purification offerings (see Leviticus 4:6).

The significance of the addition of wood, hyssop and wool to the burning cow is not immediately obvious. It may be to symbolically increase the efficacy of the ashes – these are all elements used in other purification offerings, though in different ways. There then follow the cleaning up regulations. The priest is unclean until evening; so is the man responsible for burning the heifer (v. 8). Both need to wash their clothes and the ashes collector is also unclean (v. 10). Up to now, no mention has been made of what will be done with the ashes, though it will become clear from the following section that the ashes are a ready, portable and convenient supply to be mixed with water and provide a purification solution.

Instructions for using the cleansing water (19:11-22)
Verses 11 to 13 introduce the use of the water in general terms. It is to be used on the third and last days of the seven days outside the camp (5:1-4 does not specify the length of banishment). Use of the water will make the man or woman clean. Omission is serious; he or she will be 'cut off from Israel' (v. 13).

The next small section (vv. 14 to 16) introduces two particular cases: death in a tent and death in the open. Verses 17 to 21 then expand on how the ashes-in-water mix is to be administered. Note that no priest is required, only a 'man who is ceremonially clean' (v. 18). This is because the priest has already made the ashes effective by his presence at their preparation. Again, we read that this is a lasting ordinance (v. 21).

Verses 21b to 22 function as a kind of appendix. The clean man who sprinkles the water himself becomes unclean by virtue of the act. Like the priest and earlier helpers, he remains unclean until the evening. Uncleanness spreads!

From text to message

Getting the message clear: the theme
Though this provision is meant to be portable and convenient, a kind of instant-coffee type cleansing ("just add water"), the people need to understand that death is still required for cleansing. However, this provision only deals with ceremonial cleansing, cleansing that is outward. It does not and cannot deal with inward impurity.

Getting the message clear: the aim
The people cannot approach God ceremonially unclean, but the provision of cleansing in Numbers 19 is still unable to deal with the heart and 'consciences from acts that lead to death' (Heb. 9:14) leaving us crying out for a better sacrifice.

A way in
Everybody knows that however good instant coffee is, it is never as good as the real thing. It is convenient, portable and quick, but just not as tasty. It never smells as good. Death is a real problem for Israel and this clever and useful provision deals with the ceremonial problem. But it cannot address the deeper issue.

Ideas for application

+ We cannot approach a pure and perfect God without being cleansed and made pure. The primary application must be to the work of our great High Priest Jesus. As we journey, we need to remember that our access to God is always and only through his work.

+   Hebrews 9 picks up two applications:
    +   That we are saved to serve the living God (Heb. 9:14)
    +   That Jesus' death is the guarantee that we will inherit what God has promised (Heb. 9:15)

Suggestions for preaching

Sermon 1

Hebrews 9:13-14 should be the preachers' control here. 'The blood of goats and bulls and *the ashes of a heifer* sprinkled on those who are ceremonially unclean sanctify them so that they are outwardly clean. How much more, then, will the blood of Christ, who through the eternal Spirit offering himself unblemished to God, cleanse our consciences from acts that lead to death, so that we may serve the living God!' (my italics added for emphasis).

A possible sermon outline picks up on the lessons of chapter 19 and draws appropriate lines to Christ using Hebrews language and reasoning as a guide:

+   **A sacrifice that is once for all.** Unlike other sacrifices in Israel (one sin, one sacrifice, e.g. Num. 15:27-28) here is one sacrifice for many. One cow produces 4kg of ash.[3] That represents a lot of cleansing water. Once for all is an important phrase in Hebrews when considering the sacrifice of Christ (e.g. Heb. 10.10).

+   **A sacrifice that is outside the camp.** This makes the red heifer sacrifice unique. All the other sacrifices take place in the tabernacle. Remainders were burnt

---

3   I think, if I recall correctly, that the local crematorium manager once informed me that bodies reduce down to 1% ash to body weight. For a 400kg cow, this represents 4kg of ash.

outside the camp, but the sacrifice itself takes place *inside*. This offering is outside the camp from start to finish. The sacrifice is located where the problem is – outside of God's presence. Similarly, the sacrifice of Jesus takes place outside the camp (Heb. 13:11) which has a remarkably radical application, 'let us, then, go to him outside the camp, bearing the disgrace he bore' (v. 13).

+   **A sacrifice that equips us to serve and guarantees our future.** The two applications picked up by Hebrews can also be seen in the Numbers text. The cleansing water makes it possible for Israelites to come back into the camp where they can participate in the service of the living God once more. Moreover, the very nature of the portable provision makes it clear that here is a provision that Yahweh is giving his people which will go on being useful into the future as they journey.

The preacher or teacher must show that the offering of the red heifer prefigures the death of Christ.

Sermon 2
Duguid's approach is not to jump to the sacrifice of Christ quite so quickly. His outline is worth repeating:[4]

+   The need for cleansing

+   The provision for cleansing

+   Our ongoing need for cleansing, pleading Jesus

---

4   This is an abbreviated summary of chapter 24 of Duguid, p. 239

Suggestions for teaching

Questions to help understand the passage

1. Why is there a need to provide purification for uncleanness? See Numbers 5:1-3 and 16:49.

2. Note down how the ashes are prepared (vv. 2-10). What do you notice about this offering that is different from the other offerings of the covenant?

3. What happens to those who prepare the ashes and tidy up? Why?

4. How are the ashes to be used (vv. 11-19)?

5. What would be the significance of ignoring this instruction? Why?

Questions to help apply the passage

1. Read Hebrews 9:11-15. What does the writer have to say about these ashes?

2. How do the provisions of chapter 19 foreshadow the sacrifice of Christ?

3. In what way are they deficient when we think of the perfect sacrifice that is Jesus' death?

4. What is the result of having our consciences cleansed by Christ (Heb. 9:14 and 15)?

5. What does the writer say about Jesus' death being outside the camp (see Hebrews 13:11-14) and how does he apply that to the Christian life?

10
Salvation (20–21)

Introduction

For those taking a geographical approach to Numbers, chapter 20 marks the beginning of the third and last section as the people travel from Kadesh (20:1) to the plains of Moab (22:1). On this basis, these two chapters constitute a travel section, though far too much happens for them to be simply transitory. Moreover, there are common themes of rebellion and grace which demonstrate that whilst there may be a *geographic* change there is no such corresponding *spiritual* one.

So, as explained in Part 1, it is better to see these chapters as forming part of the story of the first generation. Indeed, we begin to see the death-throes of that generation in the death of, first, Miriam (20:1) and then Aaron (20:28). We also discover the reason that Moses will not be able to enter the land (20:12). This, then, is material that firmly belongs with the previous chapters.

As such, it does seem more of the same (rebellion, grumbling, intercession, grace and salvation). However, there are some important additions. First is the story of Moses himself. His refusal to 'trust' in Yahweh means he too, like his compatriots, will not be able to enter the land. Secondly, this is the first time we start to see how Israel will interact with other nations (one refusal, three battle victories). Third, the rebellion – which itself has a familiar ring (21:4-5) – is dealt with in a surprising way which is used by the Apostle John as an illustration of Jesus' crucifixion. Finally, it is in this section that we have two portions of poetry, the only time this genre breaks into Numbers in any significant way.

Listening to the text

Context and structure

Although the passage is set in a number of different places (and therefore can feel a little like a disparate collection of stories), it is primarily introduced by the death of Miriam (20:1). This is the beginning of the end – a fact confirmed by the death of Aaron and the announcement of Moses' demise. All of this first generation will fall; hence the inclusion of another grumbling section (21:4-9) which highlights the continuing rebellion of the nation.

What, though, of the other pericopes? What function do they have? The battle/nation stories (against Edom, Arad, the Amorites and the Bashanites) move the narrative of the entire book along. Though there is a distinct break between the first and second generations (marked by the census of chapter 26), it is not unexpected that as the time of the second generation nears, we begin to experience exactly what it will mean to conquer Canaan.

This, however, does still not explain the one remaining story – that of the travel section 21:10-20 and the Song of the Well (vv. 17 to 18). Previously, the desire for water nearly always resulted in grumbling (as in this section, 20:2-9). Now, the water is a gracious gift from the Lord. There is no grumbling. We are truly getting ready for a better generation than the one we have got used to so far. The narrator/editor is moving the story along and preparing us for the next generation.

The various small stories that make up the larger whole are well defined by the NIV headings:

+ Water from the rock (including the death of Miriam) (20:1-13)

+ Edom denies Israel passage (20:14-21)

+ The death of Aaron (20:22-29)

+ Arad destroyed (21:1-3)

+ The bronze snake (21:4-9)

+ The journey to Moab (21:10-20)

+ Defeat of Sihon and Og (Amorites and Bashanites) (21:21-35)

Alternatively, it is possible to see these stories as being two collections broadly following the same pattern: death (Miriam/Aaron), rebellion (both times including lack of water), confrontation (Arad/Sihon and Og).

Working through the text

Water from the rock (including the death of Miriam) (20:1-13)
This entire section will explain why the first generation leaders were not able to enter the land, starting with the one

who enjoys least coverage in Numbers, Miriam. That she is a significant person is made clear in both Exodus 15 and Numbers 12. Miriam's death receives little comment but we should not assume that as no mourning is mentioned (compare Aaron's death in 20:29), there is none.

The death announcement really serves as a little introduction to the story that follows and, once again, it is a reminder of why this generation will not enter the land. Once again the lack of water makes the Israelites grumble against Moses and Aaron. Once again they wish they were either dead (v. 3) or, at least, back in Egypt – to them the *real* land of milk and honey. This appears to be an abbreviated story because this time around there is no mention of judgement against Israel nor Moses' intercession (although the latter may be implied by verse 6). We simply read about the Lord's provision for water for the community.

Such an abbreviation is not surprising. Not only are we used by now to the pattern, we also know that such grumbling incurs God's wrath; it hardly needs to be said. However, more significantly, this is not really a passage about the people's grumbling; rather, it is about the cause of Moses' fall in the desert.

At first glance it all seems straightforward. Moses is to take his staff and 'speak to that rock' (v. 8). This is a different pattern from the previous water incident (also at a place called Meribah, see Exodus 17:1-7) and, as we shall see, the subtle changes are significant.

Moses seems to start well, 'he took the staff from the Lord's presence, just as he commanded him' (v. 9), but from then on things go awry. Rather than speaking to the rock, he speaks to the nation, a word of rebuke. The psalmist calls these 'rash words' (Ps. 106:33) which are not justified by the rebellion which 'angers the Lord' (Ps. 106:32). Moses then strikes the rock (rather than speaking to it). It is this disobedience which angers the Lord.

On the face of it, it seems a little sin and hardly worthy of the punishment it receives. However, Moses has forgotten that it is God who does the miracles, not him. 'Must *we* bring you water out of this rock?' (v. 10) (my italics added for emphasis). He did not trust the Lord enough 'to honour [him] as holy in the sight of the Israelites' (v. 12), and this is the reason for his punishment. Both Moses and Aaron have 'rebelled against [the Lord's] command' (20:24).

The Lord's instructions were very clear. Take the staff. Speak to the rock. Moses, probably in anger, took a different path. He took the staff. He spoke to the people. He struck the rock. He 'broke faith' with the Lord (as Yahweh himself later describes it – see Deuteronomy 32.51). This is no little thing.

Edom denies Israel passage (20:14-21)
The previous attempt to enter the promised land from the south (14:39-45) has been an unmitigated disaster. Now Moses tries to lead the people in from the east through Edom (another name for Esau).[1] Twice, Moses tries to negotiate safe passage. His first appeal (v. 17) must seem a little unrealistic to the Edomites; no water required! They don't, however, know about the rock! The answer is "No!" (v. 18).

The second appeal dampens the request a little – this time if they do drink water, they will pay for it (v. 19). The answer remains the same. No. It is reinforced with a large army. The implication seems to be that this is a powerful

---

1   Esau was, of course, Jacob's brother so Moses' appeal in verse 13 to 'brother' Edom is factually correct.

army, but surely not larger than the Israelite fighting force? The only explanation is that, ultimately, the Lord does not want them to be successful this way. Their forty year discipline is not yet over.[2]

What purpose does this story serve? Its inclusion is important because the next battle stories (three victories) might give the impression that the job is done and this generation *can* conquer the promised land. No, they cannot. Any victory this side of the second census will be one of God's gracious patience and will not be part of an all-conquering faithful nation. This story, at least, reminds us of that sobering truth.[3] Sandwiched between two stories of failure (first Moses, then Aaron), here is a reminder that rebellion leads to failure.

The death of Aaron (20:22-29)

Aaron's death warrants more explanation than that of Miriam. He cannot enter the land because of the shared sin with Moses; however, Aaron's judgement comes sooner than that of Moses. There are similarities with Deuteronomy 34; both deaths take place up a mountain and include reminders of the rebellion. Both are accompanied by thirty days of mourning. Both involve transfer of leadership (Aaron to Eleazar; Moses to Joshua). No such transfer was required with the death of Miriam.

Arad destroyed (21:1-3)

The fighting Israelites in chapter 21 seem to be a different nation! How can this be? It is still the same generation who

---

2   Interestingly, the text flits between using first person singular ('I') and first person plural ('we') to describe the nation, capturing the corporate identity of Israel. Our English translations do not do justice to this nuance.

3   In the broader sweep of Israel's history it is both consistent with what has gone before and what is to come (see, for example, Amos 1:11).

will fall in the desert (and those who have still to reach the nadir of rebellion in chapter 25). It is best to see the events of chapter 20 as having a significant impact upon the nation. They have seen the death of two key leaders. Probably they have heard about the demise of another. It is now apparent to them that they will not enter the promised land; if Miriam, Aaron and Moses are not to go in, what hope is there for the rest of the nation? And so, what do they have to lose?

Their first skirmish with Arad is not positive as some Israelites are captured (v. 1). But they make a vow to the Lord and the Lord listens. Israel enjoys its first battle victory since Sinai. Significantly, it is against some inhabitants of Canaan. What a difference to the first battle of Hormah! (see 14:45).

The bronze snake (21:4-9)

However, just before we get too excited (and optimistic) about this generation, we catch them grumbling again. The reader is in no doubt what to make of the nation overall. Their victories are not enough to convince us that they have finally changed. They are still the malcontents of earlier chapters.

The complaint is familiar (v. 5), this time brought on by a circuitous route that they are forced to take around Edom. As with previous patterns of rebellion, their grumbling incurs the Lord's wrath and a plague of snakes comes amongst them. There is immediate contrition and the people appeal to Moses, their intercessor, and Yahweh hears his cries. Moses is instructed to make a bronze snake and 'put it up on a pole' (v. 9). Anyone bitten by the snake can look up and live.

It is the faithful act of looking at the snake that provides salvation rather than anything inherently salvific about the snake itself. Later, Jesus adds an extra dimension to the story drawing a parallel between his own death and the 'lifting up' of the snake. 'Just as Moses lifted up the snake in the desert, so the Son of Man must be lifted up, that everyone who believes in him may have eternal life' (John 3:14-15). The story receives no other comment here in Numbers.[4]

The journey to Moab (21:10-20)

The travel section of verses 10 to 20 is unremarkable, except that it introduces the reason for the Amorites' later aggression (the Israelites have camped on their territory, verse 13). The Book of the Wars of the Lord (v. 14) is an unknown document.

Nor do we know much about the well of Beer (v. 16), other than what is recorded here: it was the place 'where the Lord said to Moses, "Gather the people together and I will give them water."' The song which the people sing as a result has more significance than praise for provision. The lack of water has been a reason for grumbling, complaint and, ultimately, judgement. It is the reason that Moses, the great leader, will not enter the land. A song of reminder about the Lord's provision of water, therefore, seems a highly appropriate way to recollect the wilderness wanderings.

---

4   It is not the last we hear about the bronze snake. By the time of Hezekiah (2 Kings. 18:4) it has a name ('Nehushtan') and has become an object of worship. The king destroys it. Therein lies an application; that good things provided by God for our benefit can easily become objects of worship in and of themselves. Protestants have long leant on this lesson to object to crosses in places of worship, for example.

Defeat of Sihon and Og (Amorites and Bashanites) (21:21-35)
The final section describes the defeat of two nations (and two kings): Sihon the king of the Amorites and Og the king of Bashan. In both cases the kings are the aggressors. In Sihon's case, he refuses passage, much as Edom did. But here, his intention seems to be more than scaring the Israelites off. He initiates battle (v. 23). Israel is victorious, up to a point, not going beyond the borders of the Amorites into the land of the Ammonites (a nation which is not finally subdued until the days of David, see 2 Samuel 8:12).

Included amongst the conquest was the city of Heshbon, the capital. This is the city which is the subject of the song in verses 27-30. The song is basically the story of Heshbon. It was from there that Sihon launched his successful (and famous?) victory against Moab. But all this is overshadowed by Israel's victory (v. 30). The thrust of the song's message is "Look how powerful Heshbon has been, conquering Moab. But we have conquered Heshbon!" And so this is the song of how Israel 'settled in the land of the Amorites' (v. 31).

Next, Moses turns his attention to Bashan (continuing the battle against the Amorites on the way). Bashan too comes out to meet Moses and engages in battle. This time Moses receives a direct communication from the Lord. He is not to be afraid but to apply the same ruthless approach that he took with the Amorites. He can do this because the Lord has 'handed him over to you' (v. 34). Victory is assured and delivered. 'And they took possession of his land' (v. 35). This is still not the promised land (Og lies 30 miles or so to the east of the Jordan river boundary). But the scene is being prepared for the second generation to come.

From text to message

Getting the message clear: the theme

Once again, an apparently disparate group of stories provides a challenge to the preacher. However, there is a clear unifying theme: the first rebellious generation is slowly coming to its promised end; even its leaders are dying. There is hope, however, as the text anticipates the success of the second faithful generation to come and points towards a future event which will provide full and final salvation.

Getting the message clear: the aim

The text, not for the first time, illustrates clearly the nature of sin and grace. Christians need to understand the corruption of the flesh and the wonder of the gospel. Mercifully, in Christ Jesus, the latter trumps the former: 'O Jesus, full of grace and truth, more full of grace than I of sin.'[5]

A way in

What do you expect when the odds are stacked against you? For some congregations, a sporting illustration might work (although the preacher should take care not to use these too often). A political illustration might also suffice. All the evidence up until now is that the people of God are in self-destruct mode. Even their leaders rebel. Can God's grace possibly triumph in the end? What hope is there for the people of God?

Ideas for application

- The passage paints a bleak but realistic picture of the human heart and its tendency to sin.

---

5   This hymn by Charles Wesley is sometimes known by its rarely used first line 'Weary of wandering from my God', see http://nethymnal.org/htm/w/e/wearwfmg.htm. Accessed 12 September 2012.

+ This is set in tension with the grace of God displayed through continued provision, victory and salvation from deserved judgement.

+ We must not think that one or two victories on the journey prove that we have reached perfection.

+ The God-given snake lifted up paints a clear picture of the Messiah who will be similarly lifted up on the cross (see John 3:14).

Suggestions for preaching

This is one of the most difficult sections to preach in one unit, being made up, as it is, of many stories. Some suggestions for breaking down the text into smaller units will be made below. However, the provision of water does link the stories together, featuring as it does in the rebellion of 20:1-13, the request for passage in 20:14-21, the second rebellion in 21:4-9 and the celebration song in 21:17-18.

A sermon on this entire section will not be able to pick up on every detail. However, it will paint the broad pictures that the text warrants.

Sermon 1

This suggestion picks up on the broadest of themes and teaches God's people about the nature of sin and salvation.

+ **The all-encompassing nature of sin.** Sin is painted at its blackest here. Much can be said about:
  + the recurring nature of sin (the rebellion passages of 20:2-5 and 21:4-5) are sobering in their familiarity.
  + the reach of sin. Miriam and Aaron's deaths are reminders of the long reach of sin even to God's appointed leaders. This is reinforced by Moses' own sin in 20:9-12.

   ✦   the devastating effect of sin. The wages of sin is death
       (21:6, Rom. 6:23). Who can say that the plague of
       snakes as punishment is unjust or unwarranted?

The passage paints a blackness that God's people need
to see and understand, not least in their own hearts. The
world tempts us to think of sin lightly both in terms of the
way it spreads and the end results it can bring.

   ✦   **The all-conquering ministry of grace.** Standing in
       contrast to the people's sin is the grace of God displayed
       in provision (20:11 and 21:16-18) and battle victory
       (21:1-3 and 21:21-35). Both are needed if the people
       of God are to make it out of the wilderness. Both of
       these two wonderful gifts are celebrated in song: the
       song of the well (21:17-18) and the song of victory
       (21:27-30, quoted loosely in Jeremiah 48:45-46).
       However, it is in the provision of the bronze snake
       that Yahweh's grace is most clearly demonstrated as he
       saves his people from deserved judgement and death.
       No wonder this serves as an illustration in John's
       gospel of the triumph of grace over sin.

Sermon 2

Moving more slowly, the rebellion of Moses (20:1-13)
is worthy of a sermon in itself. It is picked up in both
Deuteronomy 32 and Psalm 106. The failure of Moses,
possibly *the* preeminent man of God in the Old Testament,
is made more stark because Yahweh has already endorsed
him as being out of the ordinary (see 12:3-8). It might be
tempting to make this into a message about leadership (and
there would presumably be some valid application there),
but it is more faithful to the text to see similar points to those
made above – namely, that Moses' rebellion demonstrates

how far sin can reach and the effect it can have (failure to inherit, made clear by his brother's death in the following story). However, in this case grace is seen in the one whom Moses foreshadows. Moses is a descendant of the first Adam. Christ is the perfect man, a second Adam, who does for us what Moses could not do for himself.

Sermon 3

The story of the well (21:10-20) is remarkable in that many of the rebellion passages in Numbers centre on the people grumbling for water. Two such passages occur in this section alone. Most of these follow the same pattern: the people gather together and grumble to Moses (and thus, to the Lord) about their lack of provision. Here, the situation is reversed. Though the story of the well has not been preserved, we do know that this is where the Lord said to Moses, 'Gather the people together and I will give them water' (v. 16). Sandwiched as it is between two travel accounts (21:10-13 and 21:18-20), we see a picture of a gracious God providing for his people so that they can journey towards the promised land. Paul's assessment that the people 'drank from the spiritual rock that accompanied them and that rock was Christ' (1 Cor. 10:4) brings this provision of grace into sharp focus for the Christian.

Suggestions for teaching

Questions to help understand the passage

1. Why does the passage mention the death of both Miriam and Aaron (20:1 and 20:22-29)?

2. Why will Moses also die in the wilderness? What does he do wrong in 20:2-13? Look up Deuteronomy 32:48-52 and Psalm 106:32-33.

3. What causes the people to grumble yet again? See 21:4-5.

4. How does the Lord respond this time?

5. What salvation does the Lord provide when the people repent? See 21:8-9.

6. Given all the grumbling about water, what is the significance of the song of the well in 21:10-20?

7. Why, given all their rebellion, are the people of God suddenly victorious in battle in 21:21-35?

Questions to help apply the passage

1. What do the various stories teach us about sin and its consequences? Think about whom it affects and the consequences to which it leads.

2. We know this generation will all die in the wilderness, but in this particular section, which triumphs: sin or grace? What is the evidence for your answer?

3. How does the Apostle John interpret the snake in John 3:14? How does that begin to help us understand how sin is dealt with by the cross of Christ Jesus?

4. What happens to the snake and what lessons can we draw from its history? [See 2 Kings 18:4][6]

5. How does the triumph of the cross over sin help us to fight indwelling or recurrent sin?

---

6   Depending on your group, this question may be an unnecessary diversion, use with care.

11
BLESSING (22–24)

Introduction

Until the *Shrek* movies burst onto the scene in 2001, talking donkeys were few and far between. Ask someone what they know about Numbers and it may well be to these chapters that they refer. Everyone's heard about the talking donkey!

She (and, unusually, the donkey is a she) only speaks for three verses, but for many the image dominates this section. That is something of a shame because the text functions in an unique way in Scripture and too much discussion about whether donkeys are *able* to speak or not detracts from what is really going on.

From time to time, Scripture pulls back from a close focus on the people of God and looks at what is going on in the enemy camp. This happens in Herod's Jerusalem court in Matthew 2, for example. However, most of the time we know about enemy activity in just a few passing verses or when one of our heroes gets to hear news; this is what happens to Gideon who overhears the Midianite soldiers in Judges 7:13.

Numbers 22–24 is something quite different. It is an extended focus on the enemy camp detailing what is going on as the people march by, at this stage completely unaware of what is happening with Balak and Balaam. The fact that it is included in Scripture tells us that the Israelites eventually found out what had happened (through Balaam himself, in all probability). And its inclusion here functions as a message of confidence and assurance to a beleaguered people.

Their own propensity, as we have seen, is to self-destruct and, if it wasn't for the grace of God they would surely all have suffered the fate of Korah. However, God's grace not only preserves the nation but is working behind the scenes to bless them. God's blessed people cannot be cursed and if we were in any doubt that this is the theme of the section it is a refrain that is repeated in 22:12, 23:8, 23:20 and 24:9.

How encouraging it should be for the people of God to know that, behind the scenes and away from our sight, God is on our side and the blessings we enjoy from being in Christ cannot and will not be removed.

Listening to the text

Context and structure

Balaam actually utters seven oracles in this passage. However, it is best to see the structure around the various scenes that play out rather than using the oracles to divide the text.

+ Scene 1: Balaam summoned (22:1-14)

+ Scene 2: Balaam summoned again (22:15-20)

+ Scene 3: Balaam journeys to see Balak (22:21-35)

+ Scene 4: Balaam's first oracle (22:36–23:12)

+ Scene 5: Balaam's second oracle (23:13-26)

+ Scene 6: Balaam's third oracle (23:27–24:14)

+ Scene 7: Balaan's other oracles (24:15-25)

As before, this is a lot of material for one sermon, but there is also a common theme that runs through all the oracles and this must not be lost by splitting the text up. The story of Balaam does not actually finish at 24:25 because the whoring of the Israelites in chapter 25 is a direct result of his intervention (see 31:16).

It also appears – on a first reading, perhaps – that the text is a little enigmatic about whether we should consider Balaam one of the good guys or the bad guys. It is best to see how Balaam is treated in the whole of Scripture when coming to a conclusion. There we can see that Balaam is far from being a hero. He is greedy, arrogant and finds other ways to plot the nation's downfall. This makes sense of some of the negative clues that are scattered throughout these chapters. However, we must also acknowledge that the oracles he speaks are genuine. Perhaps, like Caiaphas the High Priest, he 'did not say this on his own' (John 11:51).

Working through the text

Scene 1: Balaam summoned (22:1-14)
The story begins with a strong link to the previous section. Not only does it record the movement of Israel (v. 1), but it relates that Balak (who is king of Moab, see verse 4) is terrified at the prospect of meeting the nation, given the destruction that they have wreaked upon the Amorites (21:25). Remember that the Amorites had previously

defeated the Moabites (21:26) in great displays of power; Balak was right to be scared, 'Indeed, Moab was filled with dread because of the Israelites' (v. 3). Israel's destruction of Moab would be total (v. 4).

What does a pagan king do in such circumstances? He calls for the seer and pays for a curse. His only hope against such overwhelming and proven military might is to resort to spiritual powers that he hopes he can access. So enters Balaam into the story. Balak hopes that Balaam will 'put a curse on these people because they are too powerful for me. Perhaps then I will be able to defeat them' (v. 6).

Balaam clearly has a reputation in this area (v. 6) and so is a natural choice. But what exactly is his status before Yahweh? There certainly seems to be some evidence of a real relationship, after all he speaks to the Lord and the Lord replies (v. 8). He knows the divine name for God. But he cannot have been a great devotee of Yahweh because he takes part in pagan rites (22:40–23:3, 23:14-15) and he looks for omens (24:1, ESV), both clearly forbidden in the law. Nonetheless, he does have some knowledge of Yahweh (perhaps left over from the time of the Patriarchs?). Most likely, his religion is a mish-mash of truth and untruth.

This section of Numbers moves away from exclusive use of the divine name, Yahweh. God is also addressed here as God (using both *elohim* and *el*) as well as the name *shadday* and even a more pagan name *elyon*. The only part of the story where the name Yahweh dominates is in the story of the donkey. But it is difficult to draw any certain conclusions from this information. Whilst the text remains a little ambiguous about the precise nature of the relationship, there is no doubt that Balaam does speak Yahweh's true word.

Balaam's initial reaction, after consultation with the Lord, is that he should not heed Balak's summons (v. 12). Everything seems above board and there, we might have thought, the story should end.

Scene 2: Balaam summoned again (22:15-20)
Balak however has no other cards to play and so he persists with Balaam sending 'other princes, more numerous and more distinguished than the first' (v. 15). We might expect a faithful follower of Yahweh to refuse this revised appeal. After all, the Lord is clear, 'you must not put a curse on these people, because they are blessed' (v. 12). That fact will not change should even Balak himself come and do the pleading.

There is a change in approach in this second request, however. Previously the elders have brought 'the fee for divination' (v. 7). Now they promise the earth; Balaam will be 'rewarded handsomely' (v. 17). Balaam's approach *sounds* very godly. He cannot do anything beyond the command of the Lord. Nevertheless, there is a chink in his armour. The language of verse 19 is significant, 'Now stay here tonight as the others did, and I will find out what *else* the Lord will tell me' (italics added for emphasis). The Lord's previous answer should have told him that there is nothing else to be said.

It is in this context that we need to read the Lord's answer. Note, I think significantly, that whenever God speaks to Balaam in this section he is not described with the divine name. Unlike Moses ('And the Lord spoke'), it is 'God' who speaks to Balaam despite the fact that he enquires of 'the Lord.' And this time around, God's reply is that Balaam should go.

What are we to make of the divine condescension? Has God changed his mind? That hardly seems likely. More obviously, it is the sin of Balaam (which the New Testament identifies as greed, see 2 Peter 2:15-16, Jude 11, Rev 2:14) which has led Balaam to "double-check" with the Lord. More is now on offer, perhaps God will let him go after all? This is Balaam being given up to his sin. God's permission is therefore not a word of grace but one of judgement.

Scene 3: Balaam journeys to see Balak (22:21-35)
So Balaam departs[1] and God is angry. Why, though, is he angry given that Balaam seems to be doing precisely what the Lord has commanded? The ESV seems to link God's anger with his travelling, 'But God's anger was kindled *because* he went' (v. 22, my italics). The Hebrew word *ki* is common enough (over 650 occurrences in the Old Testament) and most of the time 'because' is a good translation. However, it can also mean 'when' – in other words, it can have a temporal meaning as well as a causal one.[2] This is the approach of the NIV translators who render verse 22, 'But God was angry *when* he went.'

On this basis there is still no explanation for *why* God is angry, but at least there isn't the immediate conflict with

---

1   This text (Num. 22:21) gives rise to one of the best known stories about preaching. D Martyn Lloyd-Jones recalls hearing a preacher who was wedded to three headings. So, for this text he took (1) *A good trait in a bad man*, as Balaam rose early. (2) *The antiquity of saddlery* for the passage demonstrates that it is 'neither modern or new, but an ancient craft' and (3) *A few remarks concerning the woman of Samaria*. The preacher could think of nothing else to say. So, says Lloyd-Jones, headings should be 'natural and appear to be inevitable.' We might add that preachers need not be slaves to having three points, nor should they take such short texts that they lose sight of the setting and main point being made. See D Martyn Lloyd-Jones, *Preaching and Preachers* (London, UK: Hodder & Stoughton, 1971), p. 208

2   For example, Job 13:9

verse 20. For an answer to the first part of that question we need look no further than the next few verses where the Lord makes it clear that Balaam's path is 'reckless' and deserves the punishment of death. He should have heeded the Lord's first answer and though the Lord has given him up to his desires, the anger of the Lord still burns.

Verses 23 through to 35 describe the infamous incident with the donkey. We need to say right away that it is very rare for animals to speak in Scripture. In fact, only the donkey and the serpent (Gen. 3) do so. However, the God who sends ten plagues upon Egypt, who parts the Red Sea, who destroys the Egyptian armies, who miraculously provides for 2½ million in the desert, who causes water to come from a rock (need we go on?) is hardly powerless to put words in the mouth of an ass. It would not be improper to ask someone who doubted such a thing whether they had been paying attention so far!

The story with the donkey is carefully structured. Three times an angel blocks the way. Three times Balaam is blind to the risk. Three times the donkey sees the risk. Three times the donkey tries to avert the danger. Three times Balaam hits the donkey. Within this pattern of threes there is also escalation. The first time the donkey simply turns into a field. On the next occasion the path is walled in and the donkey presses against the wall. On the third there is nowhere to turn, so the donkey simply sits down.

The story is also full of delicious irony. The paid seer cannot see what the female animal can! (The gender accentuates the irony; most Bible donkeys are male.) Some seer Balaam is! We're not meant to think well of Balaam at this point! Moreover, he strikes the donkey and wishes he could do worse and kill her (v. 29) even though it will later transpire that this animal has saved Balaam's life (v. 33). There is also symmetry in the way 'the Lord opened the donkey's mouth' (v. 28) and 'the Lord opened Balaam's eyes' (v. 31).

It *is* a funny story, by which we mean it is *meant* to make Balaam an object of ridicule and make us realise that he is not the wholesome godly servant of Yahweh we might otherwise mistake him for. Nevertheless, he is repentant (v. 34) and he offers to return. But God's sovereign purpose is that Balaam will go and show to Balak (and eventually all the world) that his blessed people cannot be cursed.

Scene 4: Balaam's first oracle (22:36–23:12)

Balak is not happy about the delay which is presumably related to the first visitation (v. 7). With his pagan way of thinking he assumes that it is because Balaam doubted his ability to recompense him. 'Am I not really able to reward you?' (v. 37). Balaam skirts the question and says, in effect, let's get on with it whilst still explaining (truthfully) that he can only speak what God puts in his mouth. The question is, what will God put in his mouth? We already know the answer (look back to verse 12), but the scenes that follow will unpack that a little.

First, there is a ritual feast. The word for 'sacrificed' can simply mean 'kill for food' (see, for example 1 Samuel 28:24) but the sense is probably right here. The whole episode is full of pagan ritual and it would be normal for the first night feast to follow the same pattern. Either way, Balaam willingly participates and the scene is set.

The first three oracles each begin the same way. At Balaam's instruction, Balak builds seven altars and sacrifices seven bulls and seven rams. These offerings seem to have the semblance of authenticity; they are described using a technical Hebrew word meaning 'burnt offering' (translated in ESV, but not NIV). Then Balaam leaves Balak and meets with God. We should not think that Balaam's plea (v. 4) meets with approval. In fact, the Lord is silent about what Balaam has done. However, he does give Balaam a message which is contained in verses 7 to 10. It consists of an introduction followed by seven couplets each of which is a mini Hebrew parallelism. The overall sense is clear. 'How can I curse those whom God has not cursed?' (v. 8a).[3]

Balak's reaction is not surprising (v. 11). He has paid the fee, why should he not expect the prophet-for-hire to deliver? But Balaam can only speak 'what the Lord puts in his mouth.'

Scene 5: Balaam's second oracle (23:13-26)
Balak now thinks that the problem is that Balaam is distracted by the sheer numbers of Israelites just as he himself was earlier (22:3). Perhaps if Balaam can only see a part of the nation then he will curse on demand? Balaam and Balak go through the same sacrificial ritual (though this time Balaam does not boast about the sacrifices to the Lord). Again, he is given a message to speak.

This time the message is longer. Balaam first addresses himself to Balak himself and announces the character of God to the pagan king (vv. 18 and 19). Although a word from Balaam to Balak, it is clearly a word that he has been commanded to speak, it is part of his 'oracle.' Essentially it tells Balak what the readers of Numbers already know. God keeps his promises. He will neither change his mind nor fail

---

3   The phrase 'live apart' in verse 9 is worthy of further comment. In the Old Testament it can either mean living alone (for security or safety) as in Deuteronomy 33:28 or it can mean chosen or elect, as in Exodus 19:5. Perhaps both are in view here?

to act upon what he has said he will do. Balak should not expect a change.

And neither does he get one in the main body of the oracle (vv. 21 to 24). However, this time the words go further. Whereas before they confirmed that the nation was blessed, here the blessing is spelt out in more detail, and it is not what Balak wants to hear. For Israel, blessing means that the Lord is with them; he has made them victorious in battle and he will continue to do so. 'The people rise like a lioness; they rouse themselves like a lion that does not rest till he devours his prey and drinks the blood of his victims' (v. 24). This is precisely what Balak had been afraid of (22:4).

His response is desperate. It is to stick his fingers in his ears and say, in effect, 'Shut up!' But once again the seer reminds Balak of what he has been saying all along, 'All that the Lord says, that I must do' (v. 26, ESV).

Scene 6: Balaam's third oracle (23:27–24:14)
Balak has no other option but to pursue his foolhardy quest. Fighting is out of the question. Perhaps, just perhaps, one more attempt at a curse? Once again he builds the altars at Balaam's request. He has not heard, or at least not understood, what Balaam has been saying. Unlike pagan gods who could be cajoled and persuaded to change their minds, the Lord does not lie, nor change his mind.

We get here an interesting editorial detail about Balaam. This time around (because he has seen how the Lord blesses Israel) he decides to do without the sorcery. There has been no mention of sorcery up to now, but we can see that Balaam is hardly the orthodox prophet even though the Lord is speaking through him. Here God speaks again (though this time not through a direct received word but, rather, an anointed one, much like a prophet might speak).

This third oracle steps up a gear. Not only does it come to Balaam a different way, it has markedly different content. It has an introduction which describes Balaam as the one who sees clearly (something he has not previously been able to lay claim to – see 22:31). It looks forward (whereas the other oracles were more backward focused). It is, in essence, a prophecy about Israel.

This prophecy is one of abundance, rule, power and battle victory. The images are both striking and (to an enemy) frightening. They confirm everything promised to Israel and, especially, the promises made to Abraham. It is impossible to read verse 9b without thinking of Genesis 12.

No wonder Balak is incensed. He wants to send Balaam on his way without pay; because of his messages 'the Lord has kept you from being rewarded' (v. 11). We should not think that this is an acknowledgement of the Lord. Balak is simply saying, if you get no money you've only got your 'god' to blame. Balaam seems relieved to be going and he will return to his people (v. 14). This probably means those he came from, rather than the Israelites, though we will discover in chapter 25 that he travels home via Israel's camp. So Balaam is not going to be paid, but he gives another message for free!

Scene 7: Balaan's other oracles (24:15-25)
Oracles four to seven come in quick succession in response to Balaam's dismissal. The fourth is introduced with the same words as the third. And this final prophecy about Israel 'is an extraordinary word. Not only did Balaam become the mouthpiece of God to declare the divine purpose for the chosen people, but also the vehicle of revelation of his

ultimate design in choosing them as his people, namely the preparation and coming forth of a Redeemer.'[4]

Balaam sees none other than the glorious Son of God. Perhaps, in its most immediate fulfilment it prefigures David, the one who will crush Moab, Sheth, Edom and Seir. However, it is difficult not to see the ultimate fulfilment in great David's greater son, the 'star who will come out of Jacob.'

At this point it is worth asking why this material is gathered together here. What purpose does it serve? Israel only got to hear about it later (how much later, we cannot say). How does it help them? Its meaning is quite clear. They cannot be cursed, they are God's blessed and victorious people. Moreover, Yahweh has purposed that one day a ruler will come who will be the mighty king and warrior. What confidence and hope this should give the people! What a battle cry and boost to those who have the job of subduing the land of Canaan. God is for them, who can be against them?

Certainly not the Amalekites, nor the Kenites, nor those who dwell in Asshur and Eber. Balaam utters his last three short oracles against these nations and people. The Amalekites, a constant thorn in Israel's side, were defeated by both Saul (1 Sam. 14) and David (2 Sam. 8). The Kenites will be all right; they are, after all, almost family and mostly friendly towards Israel (see, for example Judges 1:16). But their conquerors (the men from Asshur) will themselves be overcome from the marine corps of Kittim (v. 24). Taken together, these oracles are confirming the fourth oracle. Balaam is looking around from his high vantage point and

---

4   Philip, p. 242

saying, 'Not you, you or you! None of you will thwart the star coming out of Jacob.'

And so the story of Balaam ends and he returns home.

From text to message

Getting the message clear: the theme

The theme is clear: God's blessed people cannot be cursed. Balaam learns this the hard way. Balak hears but hardly seems to listen. And ultimately, this Abrahamic blessing will be fulfilled through the life, death, resurrection and reign of the star from Jacob, none other than the Lord Jesus himself.

Getting the message clear: the aim

Just as the original passage sought to give comfort and confidence to Israel, it should serve the same purpose today. We don't always know what is going on in the 'enemy camp' but we can say with confidence that as God's blessed people we cannot be cursed. We should have assurance as the church militant, marching boldly to our own promised land.

A way in

Once a preacher mentions talking donkeys many of the younger generation of listeners will be thinking of *Shrek*! It does seem something of an oddity that a donkey should speak. If you feel comfortable, you could start with a *Shrek* quote:

Donkey:	Hi Princess!
Princess Fiona:	It speaks!
Shrek:	Yes, it's getting him to shut up that's the real trick.

A talking donkey? No trick here. The Lord has done many mighty deeds and putting words in the mouth of an animal is not such a big thing. But it does show us the stupidity of Balaam. The animal sees what he cannot, but he will learn: God's blessed people cannot be cursed.

An alternative way in would be to introduce the idea of seeing into the enemy camp. That kind of intelligence is worth its weight in gold. And here is more than a glimpse into the enemy camp; it is a whole story that shows just how faithful and powerful is God's blessing on his people.

A less military illustration would be a backstage tour like one can take at the Royal Opera House or a sports stadium. It's fascinating to see behind the scenes and understand how everything works.

Ideas for application

+ God is for his people, who can be against us?

+ Even when we don't see it (or, we might add, feel it), God is working for our good. How useful to see into the enemy camp as we journey – especially as we sometimes feel we are on the losing side.

+ Ultimately, we see God working for us most clearly in the salvation he brings us through Jesus, the star of Jacob.

+ Our spiritual enemies quake in their boots at the victorious presence of the Lord with his people.

Suggestions for preaching

The length of this section again makes it a daunting prospect for a sermon, though it would be easier to digest in a bible study. I first preached this section with a guided reading (see page 53) to explain some of the detail. Then the key question to address is how does God bless us today? It is not in physical battle victory, but with the spiritual blessings we have in Christ (Eph. 1) and Christians need to be assured that these cannot and will not be removed. We cannot be cursed though the dangers along the way are many: 'trouble or hardship or persecution or famine or nakedness or danger or sword' (Rom. 8:35).

The oracles (either taken together or one by one) explain what it means to be God's blessed people, both then and now (though this side of the cross the fulfilment will work itself out differently and eternally). The preacher could pick up these oracle themes.

+ **God's blessed people enjoy God's faithfulness.** This is the point of the first oracle. Maybe Balak does not see it, but the language is similar to that of the covenant promises to Abraham. Likewise, the salvation from Egypt (second and third oracles) is about God doing what he promised to do.

+ **God's blessed people enjoy God's presence.** This becomes clear in the second oracle (23:21) and is again at the heart of a covenant relationship where God is our God and we are his people. Moses knew the importance of this presence and Numbers has made the presence of Yahweh clear.

+ **God's blessed people enjoy God's victory.** The language of battle victory is clear in each of the second, third and fourth oracles. Of course, the preacher needs to be careful here drawing direct lines from Israel to the church. The old covenant is primarily physical whilst the new is spiritual (and, therefore, better because it is lasting).

+ **God's blessed people enjoy God's abundance.** The third oracle, in particular, speaks of lush abundance. This was always a blessing of the Mosaic covenant; the blessings we have in Christ are also ones of abundance.

Each point leads us to Christ, the star who will come out of Jacob, because we enjoy all these blessings by being in him. This approach seems to make little of either Balaam, Balak or the donkey. However, that is almost certainly right. None of them is the hero of the story: Yahweh and his people feature in that exalted role. In a movie award ceremony the others would only, at best, be nominated for a best supporting role.

The section could be broken up further. However, the danger in making a shorter section focusing on chapter 22 (rather than seeing it as setting the scene for the oracles) is that the message of the oracles will quickly get lost.

Suggestions for teaching

Questions to help understand the passage

1. What prompts Balak's concern (22:1-4) and what does he hope to achieve by sending for Balaam?

2. What is Balaam's initial response and why do you think God seems to allow him to go after first refusing permission?

3. What is the *main point* of the story of the talking donkey? What does it tell us about (a) the Lord and (b) Balaam.

4. What do you make of Balaam's preparations (23:1-2, 23:14 and 23:29)? Does 24:1 throw any light on what Balaam is doing?

5. Why does God still speak through such a man?

6. What is the main thrust of the first oracle? Answer the same question for oracles two and three.

7. What is different about the fourth oracle? Whom do you suppose it is talking about?

8. Where does the action of this section take place? What part do the Israelites play in it? What purpose do you think it therefore serves?

Questions to help apply the passage

1. What kind of hardships do Christians face (look up Romans 8:35 for some help)?

2. How do the lessons of the four oracles give Christians confidence and assurance in such times? Work through your answers from questions 6 and 7 above and apply them to the Christian life.

3. Use the fourth oracle to answer where, ultimately, Christians get their confidence from.

12
SEDUCTION (25)

Introduction

The last time we encountered Israel, things were looking slightly more promising. With three battle victories under their belts (against Arad, the Amorites and Bashan) we might have thought we were finally leaving the rebellion days behind. Chapter 25 dispels any such hopeful thoughts.

In many ways it marks the low point (as well as the end point) of this first generation. Up to now their grumbling and complaining have been significant, wishing they were back in Egypt. Now we see a new dimension, worship of false gods. It is surely no accident that this is the first time in the Bible that Baal is mentioned (v. 3).

So it is best to see this last chapter as describing the death throes (literally for some) of the first generation. Perhaps, as one commentator has suggested, the plague death toll of 24,000 accounts for the very last of them?

It is also important to realise that this chapter is also the doing of Balaam. He is not mentioned in the chapter at all, and yet 31:16 sheds some light on how exactly this incident came about. The Midianite temptresses were the ones who 'followed Balaam's advice and were the means of turning the Israelites away from the Lord in what happened at Peor, so that a plague struck the Lord's people.'

Lest there be any confusion, the Midianite women punished in chapter 31 must be the same as the Moabite women of 25:1. We know this because one of the story's main characters is Cozbi. She was 'the daughter of Zur, who was the tribal head of a father's house in Midian' (v. 15). The events of chapter 25 directly lead to the battle in chapter 31: 'Treat the Midianites as enemies and kill them' says the Lord to Moses (see 25:17). Midianite and Moabite are effectively synonyms.

Listening to the text

Context and structure

The text divides neatly into two. The first section (vv. 1-5) describes Israel's seduction and the Lord's judgement. But the story is interrupted by the actions of one particularly brazen couple, Zimri and Cozbi. Their story (and their demise at the hand of Phinehas) is told in verses 6 to 18. And so ends the story of the first generation, rather fittingly with the death of two ringleaders, but also with the heroism of Phinehas, who is one of the new generation which will be counted in the second census in the following chapter.

Working through the text

Israel's seduction (25:1-5)

The action of this section takes place at Shittim, a particular place which formed part of the plains of Moab and from which Joshua will later send spies into Canaan (see

Joshua 3:1). Although there is no time marker in the text, its juxtaposition with the story of Balaam creates a sharp contrast. Whilst the Lord was blessing Israel from afar, Israel herself was practising the same self-destruction with which we've become so familiar. The similarities with the golden calf incident are obvious; as Moses was up the mountain (Balaam blesses from the mountain too), the people were 'indulging in pagan revelry' (1 Cor. 10:7).

The instigators of the rebellion seem to have been the women of Moab. This marks a change in the nature of rebellions to date, which have all been internal. Here the influences are external though, as the text will show, that does not absolve the Hebrew leaders from blame.

Two sins are interwoven and almost certainly linked. The 'men began to indulge in sexual immorality with Moabite women' (v. 1) and 'the people ate [probably participating in the sacrifices] and bowed down before these gods' (v. 2). In this way, the nation joined itself to 'the Baal of Peor.' The word for joined is repeated in the psalmist's account of the incident, but there it is translated as 'yoked' (Ps. 106:28). The latter is probably a better translation (see also ESV).

This is the first reference to Baal as a god, though the name has been used to describe a place (Exod. 14:2) and as a proper name (Gen. 36:38). Ashley explains that the name of this Canaanite god of vegetation is often associated with place names and given the definite article as here, 'the Baal of Peor.'[1] This is also how the Psalmist identifies the false deity.

It seems a supreme irony that, just as Balaam is uttering one of the most exalted messianic prophecies in the whole of Scripture so far, the Israelites are choosing that precise

1   Ashley, p. 517

moment to attach themselves to other gods. Their hearts are surely sinful through and through. We're not told much about the nature of the sexual immorality although Numbers 31:16 hints that it was a means to an end – the turning away from the living God to serve idols. This is the ultimate sin in view here, confirmed by the account in Psalm 106. No wonder that 'the Lord's anger burned against them.'

The retribution is swift and decisive as it needs to be. All the leaders are to be killed in full view of the people (v. 4, the word could also mean 'hanged'). This might seem like a harsh judgement but the whole nation has been yoked (v. 3) and the leaders are representatives of the tribes. The judges of Israel (Exod. 18, presumably a different group from the leaders) are also to extend this justice to all those in their tribes who have joined in the worshipping.

The text is silent about whether this sentence was carried out because the story is interrupted with a story within a story about two particular perpetrators and the action of Phinehas. The sentence could well have been carried out after his intervention. Part of the difficulty is that Phinehas' actions 'make atonement for the Israelites' (v. 13) but with respect to a plague that the Lord has sent among them. How can this be reconciled to the actions of verses 4 and 5?

Several explanations have been suggested. It is quite possible that the plague (first mentioned in v. 8) is the practical outworking of the burning of the Lord's anger (v. 3). In other words, the Lord's anger is not just an emotion he feels, but describes his justice running through the camp as a plague. If this is so, why are certain individuals singled out for execution? The answer must be that the public nature of their death serves as a warning. We met a similar trend in chapter 16 where Korah, Dathan and Abiram were swallowed up by the ground whilst the 250 other rebels were consumed by fire (and, later, the people were visited by a plague from the Lord).

On this reading the judgement is a plague (on the people), but the leaders are singled out for particular public punishment, as are the chief worshippers from each tribe. Ashley suggests that the public executions were not carried out and that this may be the reason for the plague[2] but this seems a less likely scenario than that outlined above.

Either way, the reader is in no doubt about the seriousness of the immorality and idolatry of the nation, a point that the psalmist is quick to make: 'They yoked themselves to the Baal of Peor and ate sacrifices offered to lifeless gods; they provoked the Lord to anger by their wicked deeds, and a plague broke out among them' (Ps. 106:28-29). Likewise, Paul makes this one of his key teaching points, 'We should not commit sexual immorality as some of them did' (1 Cor. 10:8).[3]

Phinehas' righteousness (25:6-18)
Into the story breaks the rather gruesome account of Phinehas. Before we get too squeamish and superior, however, we should remember that the highly sexual and idolatrous rebellion should make us feel *more* squeamish

---

2   Ashley, p. 521

3   There is a difficultly in 1 Corinthians where Paul lists the number of dead at 23,000, 1,000 short of the Numbers total. 'Commentators have exhausted their ingenuity in trying to explain the numerical discrepancy' [A.C. Thiselton, *The First Epistle to the Corinthians : A commentary on the Greek text* (Grand Rapids, USA: Eerdmans, 2000) p.739.] Calvin suggests that 'it is easy to reconcile them' arguing, in essence, that Moses rounded up and Paul rounded down [John Calvin, *Calvin's Commentaries: 1 Corinthians* (Albany, USA: Logos Library System, 1998 electronic edition)]

and offended than Phinehas' righteous reaction. The sin made the Lord's anger burn. And it also made the anger of Phinehas burn.

The particular incident that incurs Phinehas' wrath is that of (at this stage) an unnamed Israelite man and a Midianite woman. We will later discover that both are from privileged positions, both the children of leaders (v. 14). We need to understand that they act out their sin in the most brazen fashion. It is whilst the sentence is being pronounced on the rebels and after the plague has started that Zimri (for that is his name) brings his Midianite sexual partner Cozbi (for that is hers) to his tent.

Worse, though, he does so in full view of both Moses and 'the whole assembly of Israel while they were weeping' (v. 6). At this stage the nation are showing, at the least, remorse for what has happened. But not Zimri; his sin is definitely like that described back in 15:30 – this is defiant sin. This is Zimri taking his mistress to bed in full view of the nation; there is no shame.

Phinehas *does* see the shame and takes action. He is the son of Eleazar and the grandson of Aaron (by now, dead). He firmly belongs to the new generation and displays his credentials by taking a spear and driving it through both their bodies. Although the text is silent, the strong implication is that the spear kills them both in the act of copulation, one on top of the other. As with previous action on the part of a priest (see, for example, 16:46-50) the action is effective in turning aside the anger of the Lord.

Phinehas' actions are commended by the Lord 'for he was as zealous as I am for my honour among them, so that in my zeal I did not put an end to them' (v. 11). He thus enjoys a special covenant with the Lord, a covenant of peace. The exact nature of this covenant is then explained. Phinehas and his descendants will enjoy a covenant of 'lasting priesthood.' This might, at first, appear to mean that priests will always come from this line of Aaron. However, his uncle Ithamar also fathers a line of priests (see 1 Chron. 24:1).

Two explanations of this covenant are possible. One is that although priests came from both lines, the line of Phinehas was favoured (and that is the strong implication of 1 Chron. 24:4 which tells us that the ratio of leaders in Eleazar's line was 2:1 that of Ithamar). A more probable alternative is that the high priests would come from Phinehas' line, a strong likelihood given the list in 1 Chronicles 6:4-15 which contains some of the well-known high priests.

Psalm 106 sheds a little more light on the covenant. 'But Phinehas stood up and intervened, and the plague was checked. This was credited to him as righteousness for endless generations to come' (Ps. 106:30-31). The Abrahamic phrase (Gen. 15:6) is enormously important in understanding the nature of faith in the Old Testament. However, the psalmist seems to ascribe the credit to Phinehas' action rather than his faith. But reading the two passages together makes sense of the situation. We know that Phinehas is motivated by zeal for the Lord's honour. He *does* have faith and treasures the name of Yahweh above all else. His actions flow from that faith and it is in this way that he becomes one of the Old Testament heroes of the faith with his faith credited to him as righteousness.

The story is not quite over. First we discover the identity of the two high handed sinners. That they are both children of leaders shows how far the corruption of verses 1 to 3 has spread. In particular, Zimri, a son of a leader, should have known better but defied the Lord with his brazen immorality.

Second, there are implications of this event for the Midianite people. Both the original seduction and the actions of Cozbi have effectively made them enemies of Israel. If this incident had not taken place, we might assume that they could have been left alone; after all, the Midianites were close to family. But whether or not this might have happened, after the rebellion there is no doubt as to their fate and it is notable that the first battle of the new generation (and the only battle in the second section of Numbers) is to act out the Lord's revenge on the Midianite people.

From text to message

Getting the message clear: the theme
So near to the promised land and with God working behind the scenes to ensure they are blessed; but the people's capacity for self-destruction is seemingly without end. God's blessed people cannot be cursed but they can be seduced and the end result is equally destructive.

Getting the message clear: the aim
Paul makes the aim for us very clear, 'Do not commit sexual immorality as some of them did' (1 Cor. 10:8) but this comes as part of the broader exhortation, 'therefore, my dear friends, flee from idolatry' (1 Cor. 10:14). These commands fit neatly with the details of the story.

A way in
Although interesting to see what happens backstage, what really counts is the action on the platform. You can have all the technical wizardry, state-of-the-art equipment and perfect sets, but if the actors fluff their lines then the play is a disaster. So, the final test is to see whether the Lord's

blessing prompts the Israelites to act in a different way. Will this first generation redeem themselves at the last minute? From our reading of Numbers so far we expect not and, sadly, our expectations are fulfilled.

An alternative way in would be to consider Balaam. His plans (and that of his paymaster Balak) have come to nothing. Or have they? What if there is another way for Balaam to wreak havoc? Sadly there is, and Balaam knows it.

Ideas for application

+ The passage is clear about the danger of outside influences. Whilst Christians must not cut ourselves off from the world, we need to be realistic about the dangers it can present. The reality of our journey is that we must travel surrounded by seductive influences.

+ Neither the Lord's blessing on our journey nor his guaranteed victory makes us immune from temptation; nor do they allow us to sin with impunity.

+ Idolatry and sexual immorality are two particularly dangerous and destructive temptations.

+ We stand in constant need of the one who will turn aside the wrath of God – Jesus, the Saviour.

Suggestions for preaching

Sermon 1

This sermon completes the story of the first generation. As such, the details of the narrative are downbeat and the drama serves as a warning. Nevertheless, Phinehas (although ruthless in his pursuit of God's holiness) comes across as a ray of hope for the next generation. This may be a good point to question which generation we are more like? The passage teaches us the reality of our own hearts:

+ **Our capacity for self-destruction.** It is whilst God is blessing the people backstage that they are fluffing their lines on it. Any Christian knows the capacity he or she has for self-destruction through ongoing or recurring sin. It may be that sexual immorality is not the sin that could make us fall but we can be sure Balaam would have been able to think of something. And at the root of all sin is idolatry and turning our back on the living God. We will be unable to grow as Christians until we can understand our utter helplessness apart from Christ and the work of his Spirit.

+ **Our need for atonement.** The passage makes clear that sin cannot be swept under the carpet. Phinehas knows that atonement must be made, something must be done. And though we could call his actions harsh by today's standards, who can say that they were unfair or unjust? These two leaders' children had openly defied the Lord. Only death can turn away the righteous anger of the Lord. All of our sin must be paid for and the only question is 'who will pay?' Will it be us or will it be Christ?

+ **Our call to ruthless battle.** We must not think we can sin with impunity because Christ has died. We are called to join a ruthless battle against sin. Sin is our enemy just as the Midianites made themselves Israel's enemy. We need to be careful drawing lines from the Old Testament to the New, but we can say that we need to battle against the influence of sin in our own lives and in our churches; it must be put to death by the Spirit working in us (Rom. 8:13); that is a mark of being a child of God.

Perhaps we could also make something of the facilitator? Clever, clever Balaam! Clever, clever Satan, we could say. He knows how to make us fall and delights in it. But our encouragement is that 'when you are tempted, he [God] will also provide a way out so that you can stand up under it' (1 Cor. 10:13). Christ is both our atoning sacrifice for sin and, by his Spirit, the way we battle and stand victorious against its ongoing influence.

Sermon 2
Raymond Brown picks up separately on the motivation and action of Phinehas with a good outline:

+ Phinehas was obedient to God's word

+ Phinehas was zealous for God's name

+ Phinehas was committed to God's service[4]

Suggestions for teaching

Questions to help understand the passage

1. Who is behind the seduction of Israel in chapter 25 (look at 31:16 for help)?

2. Why is this different from all the other rebellions we have seen so far?

3. Who is ultimately responsible (see vv. 4 to 5)?

---

4   Brown, p. 232

4. What is particularly shameful about the actions of the couple in verses 6 to 9? Who are they (see vv. 14-15)?

5. How does Phinehas stop the plague and deliver judgement? Was he right to do so?

6. What does God think of his action? (See also Ps. 106:30-31).

7. What does the Lord tell Moses should happen to the Midianites as a result (vv. 16 to 18)? Why?

Questions to help apply the passage

1. What is the significance of this passage coming right after chapters 22 to 24?

2. What kinds of things seduce Christians and why?

3. What does the passage tell us about the need for atonement? Is all sin dealt with by God in this way? How can we then avoid his judgement?

4. What motivated Phinehas and how should such motivation shape our actions today?

5. What enemies should Christians be putting to death and how? You might like to read Romans 8:12-17 for help.

Part 3
LIFE IN THE PROMISED LAND
(NUMBERS 26–36)

I
BEGINNINGS (26–30)

Introduction

Chapters 26 to 30 of the book of Numbers represent a long passage which starts off the story of the second generation. As such, we get sections which seem familiar – the census count, laws about offerings, Sabbaths and festivals, and rules about vows. Nothing seems particularly new.

However, it is important for the preacher to communicate that this section *is* new. It is not simply a restatement of the old laws, but a reshaping of laws and regulations suitable for a new, godly, faithful generation who will inherit the land. We have moved from the story of the first generation who die in the wilderness to the story of the second generation who will live in the promised land that their parents rejected.

Nowhere is this transition seen more clearly than in the story of Zelophehad's daughters. This is such a significant story of the second generation (and the story continues in chapter 36) that it is worth taking as a separate sermon. These five women turn out to be the faithful believers of the book of Numbers, and – given how few faithful heroes or heroines there are – are worthy of careful attention.

This chapter, then, focuses on the whole section, but with only brief mention of 27:1-11. We will return to the daughters of Zelophehad on page 233.

Listening to the text

Context and structure

The second census serves as a clear marker that we have moved from the story of the first generation to that of the second. The story of the first has ended ingloriously, at something of a low point. The counting of the new generation – on broadly the same basis as before, introduces us to a new people, markedly different from those who have gone before. We have been prepared for this moment by occasional highlights – hints here and there that something better is on the way, together with stories like those of Phinehas in chapter 25 (who is himself a member of this second generation, even though his story comes earlier).

The structure is again straightforward:

+ The second census (26:1-65)

+ Zelophehad's daughters (27:1-11)

+ New leaders for Israel (27:12-23)

+ Rules about offerings (28:1-15)

+ Festival rules (28:16–29:40)

+ Women and vows (30:1-16)

Working through the text

The second census (26:1-65)
The second census is introduced as a new event following on from the judgement that has preceded it: 'after the

plague' (v. 1). However, it follows a recognisable pattern with much symmetry to chapter 1. The count is still a military one (v. 2). This time around, however, there is more detailed information about particular clans – only hinted at in 1:2. The additional clan information is almost certainly included to reinforce the point that some clans have suffered judgement (see 26:9-10). Once again, the Levites are not counted.

It is interesting to compare the two counts. The data are given to us so it seems sensible to see what has happened:

Tribe	First census Numbers 1	Second census Numbers 26
Reuben	46,500	43,730
Simeon	59,300	22,200
Gad	45,650	40,500
Judah	74,600	76,500
Issachar	54,400	64,300
Zebulun	57,400	60,500
Manasseh	32,200	52,700
Ephraim	40,500	32,500
Benjamin	35,400	45,600
Dan	62,700	64,400
Asher	41,500	53,400
Napthali	53,400	45,400
Total	603,550	601,730

Most noticeable are the changes to the tribe of Simeon (-37,100) and that of Manasseh (+20,500). Some commentators want to analyse these changes in light of the various rebellions that have taken place in the first half of the book. Preachers should avoid this temptation! Every one of the 603,550 men in the first column have died in the wilderness – the judgement has been total. That is not the reason that the changes have occurred.

Note that the order of the two half tribes has been reversed (compare 1:32-35 with 26:28-37). This is probably because of the size changes.

The point of comparing the two censuses is to see the remarkable truth that the total has, largely, been maintained. Given all that has taken place in chapters 1 through 25, it is astounding the men over 20 still number over 600,000. This fact points us towards the main lesson to learn from this section which is that the faithfulness of God remains unchanged and has preserved a people who are his. Frankly, this is against the human odds, as we have clearly seen.

Other points to note in this count are that the rebellion of Korah is worthy of remembrance over and above all other rebellions (see 26:8-11 and compare Psalm 106:16-18). The story of Zelophehad's daughters is also trailed by mention of their situation in 26:33 where their names are recorded for posterity in the official count lists (and not just as an adjunct story).

We should also see that this time around the count serves a secondary purpose. It is not just a list of those available to fight (though this is the initial rationale given by God to Moses and one that finds its fulfilment in chapter 31). It is also the basis on which the land will be allotted: 'The land is to be allotted to them as an inheritance based on the number of names' (v. 53).

Two explanations are given for how the land is to be divided. First, it is to be done on the basis of the count. Smaller tribes receive smaller portions; larger tribes, larger portions. But the Lord also makes it clear to Moses that lots should be drawn to divide the land (v. 55). Quite how these two work together is not made clear. Presumably the locations were chosen by lot and then adapted to reflect the size of the tribe. Thus, the allocations are both practical and fair.

This allotment, however, must not detract from the fact that the land in totality is still a gift, an inheritance (vv. 53-56, a key word which is repeated 5 times). It is the faithful God who gives the land. As before, the Levites are counted separately (vv. 57-62). They are not to receive an inheritance.

Finally, the point is made again that this count was of an entirely different generation from the census of chapter 1. 'Not one of them was among those counted by Moses and Aaron the priest when he counted the Israelites in the Desert of Sinai' (v. 64). For all the similarities to chapter 1, this is the first chapter in a new story.

Zelophehad's daughters (27:1-11)

We then meet Zelophehad's daughters more formally – their names are Mahlah, Noah, Hoglah, Milcah and Tirzah. Their names appear three times (26:33, here and 36:11). There is no son to receive the inheritance and so allowance is made for this particular family line to receive their property. The story is so significant (as indicated by the repetition of their names) that it is worthy of a separate sermon (see page 285). The inheritance of the promised land is the ultimate reward for faithfulness in Numbers.

New leaders for Israel (27:12-23)

We can be certain we are in a new generation because the leadership transfers. Moses belongs to the first generation. He will not enter the promised land because he has not honoured God as holy (a different reason from the rest of his generation, but he will still die in the wilderness). He has been a faithful leader, however, so the Lord allows him to see the promised land (27:12). This should be seen as a gracious reward rather than the way some interpret it: a rather unkind "see what you're missing because of your sin".

The actual account of Moses' death does not occur until Deuteronomy 34:4-8. This passage is not so much about his demise as about the passing of the baton to the new generation. Moses pleads with the Lord (using the same title he used back in 16:22, 'God of the spirits of all flesh') to provide a leader who will be both a warrior ('lead them out and bring them in') and a pastor ('that the congregation of the Lord may not be as sheep that have no shepherd'[1]).

The appointment of Joshua, Moses' assistant, is no foregone conclusion. He may be the natural successor (though Caleb may also have had the qualities needed), but the passage makes clear he is the man of God's choosing. The laying on of hands (vv. 18 and 23) does not impart the Spirit. The Spirit is already on him (v. 18). It signifies the transfer of leadership from Moses to Joshua.

There is a significant difference in his ministry, however. We have already seen that the relationship between Moses and the Lord was unique. The Lord spoke to Moses 'face to face, clearly and not in riddles; he sees the form of the Lord' (12:8). Joshua, however, must communicate with God in a different way.

He is to stand before the priest, Eleazar, who will inquire on his behalf using the sacred stone – the Urim (v. 21).[2] Though the precise operation is unclear, it is perfectly clear

---

1   A phrase that is picked up in both the Old Testament (Ezek. 34:5; Zech. 10:2), and the New Testament by Jesus (Matt. 9:36).

2   The Urim nearly always goes with the Thummim (except in 1 Sam. 28:6). Urim may be shorthand for both stones. Any pronouncement on how these two stones worked in practice is mere conjecture. We cannot be sure.

that the answers received through them and given to Joshua are to be as the words of God himself (v. 21).

Why the change in leadership model? Partly this may have been because Moses was a Levite and so able to enter the Tabernacle. Joshua, a member of the tribe of Ephraim (see 13:8) is not able to do this. To enter the Tent of Meeting would have meant immediate death. However, we must also assert the unique nature of Moses' ministry, pointing as it does, to that of Christ (see, for example, the Transfiguration in Matthew 17 or the comparison the writer to the Hebrews makes in Hebrews 3:1-6). This difference is made clear in the way that God speaks about 'some of your authority' in verse 20. There will not be another Moses.

Rules about offerings and festivals (28:1-15; 28:16–29:40)
We need to answer two key questions about the next two sections before we get into the detail. Firstly, why do these chapters on law, sacrifice and festivals, occur here in the text? Secondly, why are they arranged in the rather haphazard form they appear to be?

The sacrifices are about a right relationship between man who inherits the land and God who gives it. These offerings (many of which reinforce rather than transform the already existing legal system) are about maintaining that relationship. In other words, their occurrence here serves to show that God is getting the people ready for life in the land – a theme which fits well with our overall understanding of the shape of Numbers.

And the laws are far from being haphazard. In fact, the arrangement of this chapter is taken from the calendar outlined in Leviticus 23. The order moves from daily sacrifice (28:3-8) to weekly ones (28:9-10, compare Lev. 23:3), to monthly (28:11-15, compare Lev. 23:4-8) through to yearly festivals (28:16–29:38, compare Lev. 23:15-44).

In each case, we get slightly more information in Numbers than we have had before. For example, in Leviticus, the Sabbath is simply a restatement of the fourth commandment. Here in Numbers, we find the offerings that must be given each week. The feast of trumpets is instituted in Leviticus with the instruction to 'present an offering made to the Lord' (Lev. 23:25). Here in Numbers, we get the detail of what this offering entails (29:1-6).

The various offerings and festivals can be summarised thus:[3]

	Whole burnt offerings			Purification
	Bulls	Rams	Lambs	Male Goat
Daily (28:3-8)	-	-	2	-
Sabbath (28:9-10)	-	-	2	-
New Moon (28:11-15)	2	1	7	1
Unleavened bread (28:16-25)	2	1	7	1
Firstfruits (28:26-31)	2	1	7	1
Trumpets (29:1-6)	1	1	7	1
Day of atonement (29:7-11)	1	1	7	1
Tabernacles (29:12-34) Day 1	13	2	14	1
Day 2	12	2	14	1
Day 3	11	2	14	1
Day 4	10	2	14	1
Day 5	9	2	14	1
Day 6	8	2	14	1
Day 7	7	2	14	1
Tabernacles +1 (29:35-38)	1	1	7	1

---

3   This table is taken from Ashley, p. 563

Without wanting to make too much of all the details, it is immediately obvious when setting out the offerings that everything revolves around the number seven. There are seven feasts, two of which are both seven days long (Passover and Tabernacles). The seventh month has most feasts (Trumpets, Day of Atonement and Tabernacles). The number seven (or its multiple fourteen) is also obvious in the offering numbers.

Seven is a key biblical number. 'Of the numbers that carry symbolic meaning in biblical usage, seven is the most important. It is used to signify completeness or totality.'[4] This is, therefore, God himself instituting (and re-instituting) the complete system so that his people, once in the land, can relate to him, know him, love him and serve him.

Once again, the laws are not just a collection of obsolete sacrificial requirements but an eager anticipation of what is to come. These are laws for settled people; laws of abundance and generosity. They are hardly laws for travellers. The fertile inheritance is within grasp.

This is probably not the kind of commentary to analyse each festival in detail. A technical commentary on Numbers will do that better.[5] Nevertheless, one or two specific comments help draw out important points in the text:

+ The requirements for monthly offerings (28:11-15) are not found in Leviticus 23, although they are obviously already known as they appear in Numbers 10:10.

---

4   Ryken, L., Wilhoit, J., Longman, T., Duriez, C., Penney, D., & Reid, D. G., *Dictionary of Biblical Imagery* (Downers Grove, USA: InterVarsity Press, 2000), p. 774

5   For example, Ashley, pp. 555-71 or Budd, P.J. *Word Biblical Commentary Volume 5: Numbers* (Dallas, USA: Word Incorporated, 1998), pp. 309-19

+ The day of firstfruits (28:26) heralds the festival
  of weeks, also called the festival of the harvest
  (Exod. 23:16). This is the festival that later became
  known as Pentecost as it took place fifty days after the
  first grain was offered (see Leviticus 23:15-16).

+ The Day of Atonement has similarities with the
  Sabbath. On it, God's people must 'do no work' (29:7).
  The self-denial probably refers to fasting.

+ The Feast of Tabernacles (29:12-40) receives most
  attention. It is clearly designed to be a period of national
  rejoicing for all that Yahweh has done for his people. It
  is also known as the Feast of Ingathering (Exod. 23:16)
  and ends with a special day of celebration (29:35).

+ Note that we have a hint that things are returning to
  how they should be because Moses told the Israelites
  'all that the Lord commanded him' (29:40). This is not
  yet a return to the more comprehensive refrain we saw
  in, say, chapter 9:15-23, but is a clear indication that
  this generation is moving towards obedience.

Women and vows (30:1-16)
The practice of making vows is clearly an ancient one (see
the vow Jacob made in Genesis 28:20) and was mentioned
in passing in Leviticus (5:4), but this is the first time rules
about vows are codified in any detail.

The principles in this last section appear clear:

+ Men cannot break vows

+ Women can only break vows in certain circumstances:
  + A young women at home can be overruled by her
    father (30:3-5)

+ A new wife can be overruled by her husband (30:6-8)
+ A married woman can be overruled by her husband (30:9-15)

In each of the last three cases, the opportunity to be overruled is only temporary. In other words, the emphasis in the passage is not on when vows can be broken, but rather on the fact that they must, in general, be kept (reinforced in, say, verse 9 applying to widows or divorcees).

However, the last few verses of the passage make it clear that the real emphasis of this passage is not about vows at all, but about relationships between women and their men – whether fathers or husbands: 'These are the regulations concerning relationships between a man and his wife, and between a father and his young daughter still living in his house' (v. 16).

This helps answer the question as to what this passage is doing right here. Various suggestions have been made.[6] However, for our purposes it is best to go with the thrust of the text's own explanation. Like other passages in this section of the book, we have an anticipation of situations that will arise once the people are in the land, settled in homes, marrying and being given in marriage.

We can also say that there is a strong supposition here that women are able to make vows in the first place, in their own right and that such vows can only be overturned during a short period of time by a man to whom she is responsible (father or husband). The man's authority over the woman is neither absolute nor open-ended.

---

6   E.g. Wenham, p. 230 suggests four plausible reasons why this section is included here. They all seem worthy of merit.

From text to message

Getting the message clear: the theme

Like other parts of Numbers, this long section hardly seems promising material for a sermon or bible study. However, if we let the original purpose of the text drive the agenda we will discover a rich source of material. Though there are different types of writing drawn together (counts, laws, short narrative), each has the purpose of introducing us to the second generation which God will bring into the promised land.

The parallels between the first and second counts, in particular, reinforce that this section is all about *the faithfulness of God in bringing the people to Canaan*. Readers of the previous 25 chapters can be in no doubt that the people have not got here *because* of themselves, but rather *in spite* of themselves. The proper response to God's faithfulness is faith, and obedience which comes from faith (see Rom. 1:5).

Getting the message clear: the aim

We need to encourage believers with the good news of God's faithfulness to bring them to the promised land and urge them to respond in faith and obedience.

A way in

Everyone has seen pictures of – or even ridden on – old wooden rollercoasters. I grew up very near one, in the Kursaal park on Southend seafront. Riding the rollercoaster was a frightening experience. Those brave enough to attempt the ride generally expressed relief and amazement at making it to the end rather than extolling the thrill of the ups and downs.

Like an old-fashioned rollercoaster, the ride in Numbers has been up and down. Rather than getting to this point and expressing amazement at the ride, those who have stuck with Numbers should be amazed that the people of Israel have made it at all. No careful reader can assume that the people of Israel deserve victory over the Canaanites. It is clear that the victory, if it is to come, must come from God himself.

Ideas for application

+ Despite Israel's behaviour and rebellion, God has constantly remained faithful, as he continues to do with us.

+ Though our journey is replete with failures on our part, there are no failures on the Lord's part.

+ Yahweh holds out the hope and abundance of inheritance to his people, giving glimpses of life in the promised land.

+ He provides a new leader for a new generation. He will not be the same as Moses – leaving us crying out for a new Moses who will be the promised prophet.

Suggestions for preaching

Sermon 1
How do we know the faithfulness of God as we travel to our promised land?

+ **We see God's faithfulness proved in preservation** (26:1-51). Numbers started with maths and here is a repeat of the count – but with a different generation. There are individual ups and downs in the tribes (as you would expect), but overall God has preserved a people for himself. Given the rebellions, mutinies, stubbornness, grumbling, judgement and discipline (e.g. vv. 8-10), this is remarkable.

+ **We see God's faithfulness proved in promise-keeping** (26:52-65). Although the count is carried out on the same basis as before, it serves a slightly different purpose. Not only is this census for military use, but it serves as the basis for the allocation of the land (vv. 52-56). God's original promise to give his people a land and to bring them there still stands. There is a flip side, of course, because his judgement promise on oath (Ps. 95:11) is also shown to be true as none of the first generation are able to enter (vv. 64-65).

+ **We see God's faithfulness proved in provision** (27:12–29:40). The long section shows God's provision in two key ways. First, there is the provision of a new leader to replace Moses. Though Joshua will not be the same as Moses who saw the Lord 'face to face' – yet he will be one of the great warrior leaders of the people of God. Second, the various offering laws speak of a settled generation, abundantly provided for in the promised land and able to remember and celebrate the goodness of God. In these rules, we get a forward glimpse of the provision of God.

Such a sermon needs to reflect the ultimate demonstration of God's faithfulness in the Lord Jesus Christ.

It will be noticed that this outline hardly mentions chapter 30. We have seen how best to understand the chapter, but it is still difficult to fit into a sermon outline. One helpful approach might be to see it as reinforcing the response of faithfulness that is required. 'When a man makes a vow to the Lord or takes an oath to obligate himself by a pledge, he must not break his word but must do everything he said' (30:1). We have already stated that the chapter is about relationships (30:16), but these relationships are framed in terms of faithfulness to one's word, which fits neatly with the theme of God's faithfulness.

Sermon 2
I have already suggested taking the story of Zelophehad's daughters as a separate study or sermon. See page 285 for a detailed outline.

Sermons 3 and 4
Moving more slowly through the text could possibly yield more studies or sermons, though preachers or teachers would have to be careful not to lose momentum at the end of a long series. If this were done, the most natural break is to take the change-over of generations (the census and the change in leadership) as one sermon and the rules governing sacrifices as another.

On this basis, the point about God's provision and faithfulness could still be brought out in the first of two studies. The second study would need to pick up on more of the detail of the sacrifices. The best way to do this is to understand what the sacrifices entail – they are costly and abundant – and what they convey – thankfulness and repentant humility before a great God. The preacher will have to be careful not to lose sight of the context in which the laws are given.

Suggestions for teaching

Questions to help understand the passage

1. Compare 1:1-4 with 26:1-4. What are the similarities? What, if any, are the differences?

2. What is the overall change in the number of men over 20 who can serve in the army (26:51)? What does this tell us?

3. This census has a secondary purpose (26:52-56). What is it?

4. Read 27:12-23. How will Israel's new leader (Joshua) be different from its old one (Moses)?

5. Why do all the laws about sacrifices come here in the text? What do they teach us about (a) God and (b) the promised land?

6. What is the main purpose of the section on vows (see 30:16)?

Questions to help apply the passage

1. Why is the count total surprising, given the journey the people have been on so far? What does that tell us about the Lord's character?

2. Who gives the land? Why is this important to remember as we journey towards our own promised future?

3. Both Moses and Joshua have been proved to be flawed leaders in the book of Numbers. What are the people crying out for? Read Hebrews 3:1-6 to reinforce your answer.

4. What do the sacrifices teach us about the right kind of response to the faithfulness of God (see also 30:2)?

5. Now that Jesus has made the 'once for all' sacrifice for us, what does God require of us? Read Romans 12: 1-2 for help.

2

VICTORY (31)

Introduction

Chapter 31 of Numbers is the prototype battle. Many battles will be required to enter and conquer the promised land, but this is the only one set out in detail in the book of Numbers. It serves as an introduction to the way that battles *should* be fought. But the author has not just chosen a battle at random. This is the battle where revenge is sought against the Midianite/Moabite women for the seduction of chapter 25. We are left in no doubt that the holy wars fought by Israel are about exercising judgement against rebellious nations.

However, we have to admit that it is a difficult chapter to read because it is both bloodthirsty and comprehensive in its annihilation of Israel's enemies (see, for example, 31:17). It is problematic for modern readers at a number of different levels.

First, there is the question of holy war in general, of which chapter 31 is a thoroughbred example. How can a God of love sanction such wanton destruction? This is a difficult question which we will seek to answer briefly below. More detailed answers are worth searching out as this is almost certainly a question hearers and study groups will ask.[1]

The text also appears to raise additional issues, like the apparent sexual slavery of Midianite girls (31:18). A preacher or study leader will need to prepare this passage carefully to make sure he or she understands these difficult texts. Some help is included below.

However, we must not let the difficulties detract from the success of this battle. In contrast with other battles the Israelites have fought, this particular one is a model victory. Despite a bloody battle with the Midianites, not one Israelite was killed (31:49) prompting a spontaneous thank offering from the army commanders.

This battle thus sets the tone for how the Israelites are supposed to conquer the land – totally victorious, relying on their mighty God to fight with them. Of course, we know that the story does not continue this way (into Joshua and Judges).

However, the chapter is more than a battle account (though not less so). Along the way all kinds of loose ends are tied up – what happened to Balaam (Num. 22–24), how the silver trumpets work in action (c.f. 10:2-10), how soldiers deal with coming into contact with death (c.f. 5:1-4), how priests and Levites are to be provided for

---

1   There is an excellent chapter on this subject (and critiques of dissenting views) by Tremper Longman III in ed. Stanley N. Gundry, *Show them no mercy, four views on God and Canaanite genocide* (Grand Rapids, USA: Zondervan, 2003).

(c.f. 18:8-32), the reality of Moses' death and judgement on the Midianites (c.f. 25:16-18).

As such, it serves as an end marker to the whole book. Careful readers will recognise recurring themes and issues that plagued the first generation now being resolved amongst the second, faithful one.

Listening to the text

Context and structure

The context of this battle is both the death of Moses and the revenge on the Midianites for the incident at Baal-Peor (both referenced in 31:2). The chapter develops, however, into a manual for making war. So, following the battle narrative, we are told how soldiers deal with coming into contact with dead bodies (31:19-24), how to divide the spoils of war (31:25-47) and the final outcome of the battle in terms of Israelite casualties (31:48-54).

Working through the text

War against the Midianites (31:1-18)

As we have already seen in chapter 25, the Midianites are synonymous with the Moabites who engineered the downfall of so many Israelites at the infamous Baal-Peor incident. As such, this chapter is an outworking of the Lord's command in 25:17, 'Treat the Midianites as enemies and kill them...'

This is to be Moses' last act, it appears (v. 2). This does raise the question of where Deuteronomy fits into Moses' timeline. However, Deuteronomy records, in essence, Moses' final *words*. Numbers 31 records, therefore, his final *act*.

The text seems to suggest that the battle against the Midianites was a short, sharp attack rather than an all-out long-lasting campaign. This is reinforced by the fact that the Israelite army sent to do the job was relatively small compared to their total number (12,000, see 31:5) and that they killed every Midianite they found (31:7), even though the Midianite line is not wiped out (see, for example, Judg. 6:1).

The battle itself has several notable features:

+ The army is accompanied by Phinehas, son of the High Priest. He takes with him the silver trumpets (this is partly the purpose for which they were designed – see 10:1-10) and items from inside the Tabernacle. We are left in no doubt that this battle was spiritual in nature, not just physical.

+ The battle victims include Balaam along with five kings of Midian (v. 8). Nothing else is said here about Balaam, though his death is mentioned again in Joshua 13:22. It seems highly apposite that the man who engineered the downfall of chapter 25 should die alongside the Midianite rulers.

+ Initially, the army kill every man and capture every woman and child. They burn all the camps and towns (v. 10), but carry back as spoil the 'herds, flocks and goods.'

At first, this seems to be a reasonable way to wage war. However, their return is not greeted with the uniform rejoicing they might have expected. Moses and Eleazar (Joshua is strangely absent from the story) meet the returning army outside the camp (they are all unclean due to contact with dead bodies). 'Have you allowed the women to live?' (v. 15).

The army are then called to kill 'all the boys. And kill every woman who has slept with a man, but save for yourselves every girl who has never slept with a man' (vv. 17-18). This is perhaps one of the hardest statements in Numbers, and so it is worth some careful thinking.

First of all the death of the women is explained in verse 16. It is a particular judgement against the 'seduction' that chapter 25 describes and needs to be read in that light. Remember that the low point of chapter 25 includes the first mention of Baal and the first instance of the grumbling Israelites actually bowing down before an idol. This is no light thing that the women have done.

That is why the criterion for death is 'every woman who has slept with a man.' The sin at Baal-Peor was sexual (25:1) and so those who are not virgins are judged accordingly. Younger girls who are virgins are treated differently. They are spared. Verse 18 appears at first to be sanctioning some kind of sexual slavery – 'every girl who has never slept with a man' sounds to our 21st Century ears a little sordid.

However, this is simply the application of a criterion to see who is spared. There is no suggestion that the fate of these younger women would have been sexual. They were to be taken as slaves (normal practice in ancient battles).

This still leaves the question of the boys who were to be killed. Why should these young men suffer the same fate as their fathers? The answer is simple – it is the young men who would grow up to be the future warriors and avenge their parents' deaths. The Midianite line had to be wiped out. So, though barbaric to sensitive modern ears, the battle orders *do* make sense.

A preacher or group leader will need to keep in mind that the holy battles of the Old Testament are not simply about empire building but are examples of the nation acting as God's agent of judgement. All the nations ranged against the Lord deserve his wrath. That they have been spared thus far is evidence of his long-suffering. Moreover, the destruction of other nations is part of the process of removing false worship from the land (see Num. 33:52). The future history of Israel makes it clear that the failure to remove false gods from the land becomes a stumbling block for both the nation and its leaders.

Dealing with the dead (31:19-24)

Fighting raises a very practical problem for the Israelites because it is impossible to wage war without coming into contact with dead bodies. That is the nature of battle. We have already seen how Moses and Eleazar had to travel outside the camp to speak to the army.

Now the text tells us how provision is made for the soldiers to be ceremonially clean. Verses 19 to 24 explain the process by which both the warriors and the plunder they have gathered can be made clean. Now the water of cleansing which was introduced in chapter 19 comes into its own. Once purification is made, the people can come into the camp.

The spoils of war (31:25-47)

A second problem in this chapter is the vast size of the plunder: 675,000 sheep, 72,000 cattle, 61,000 donkeys and 32,000 young women (31:32-35). Some commentators worry that the numbers seem just too large. But we have to say that the numbers are possible naturally, let alone supernaturally. We don't know how many Midianites were killed, but assuming that the 32,000 young women represented, let's say, girls under 14 – then it is not unreasonable to assume that something in the region of 100,000 Midianite men or more were defeated.

On this basis, that represents just over 6 sheep per man. So, even though commentators pour scorn on the data, they are not unreasonable.[2]

This enormous spoil is divided out according to the following plan, represented here diagrammatically.

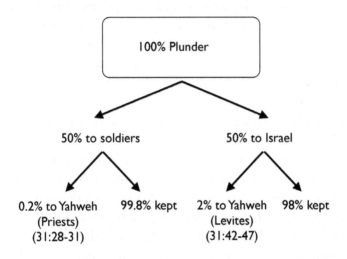

Nowhere else is this pattern repeated (for example after the battle of Jericho in Josh. 6) so it is not clear whether Numbers 31 is a special case or was designed to be normative for every battle. However, it is clear that the whole nation benefits from the victory even though the 12,000 soldiers receive the largest share. Once again, the priests and Levites are not neglected.

---

2   Wenham (p. 234) suggests that all these figures may be scaled down on the same basis as the original census – taking the word for a thousand (*elap*) to mean grouping or clan.

Giving thanks for victory (31:48-54)

We then discover the remarkable human cost of this
battle victory against the Midianites: zero. The report is
clear, 'Your servants have counted the soldiers under our
command, and not one is missing' (31:49). Again, what
seems improbable to some commentators is quite possible
when the mighty Lord of hosts fights with you and for you.

This remarkable outcome sparks a spontaneous offering
from the soldiers. This offering is entirely voluntary but
is curiously described as making 'atonement for ourselves
before the Lord' (v. 50). In what sense does it make
atonement and why is atonement needed in the first place?

Two solutions are possible. One line of thought is that
the soldiers, having seen the destruction wreaked upon the
Midianites, were overcome not only with a sense of their
own ceremonial uncleanness, but with their internalised
sin. 'As the new generation purified themselves externally
from the uncleanness of battle, they were confronted with
the reality of their own internal need for cleansing. If God
had dealt with Israel as they deserved, they themselves
could easily have been completely wiped out, just as the
Midianites were.'[3]

It is also possible that the soldiers were making
atonement for the counting – recognising that improper
and unauthorised census taking was against God's
purposes. This fits with the thrust of census atonement in
Exodus 30:11-16, even if the situation is markedly different.

Either way, the collection raises an enormous amount
of gold – 16,750 shekels is something approaching 190kg
(v. 52). The gold is brought into the Tent as 'a memorial for
the Israelites before the Lord.' It will serve as a (possibly

---

3   Duguid, p. 333

permanent?) reminder of the success of this battle and the Lord's help thus far.

From text to message

Getting the message clear: the theme

The preacher or group leader has two challenges – one is to explain carefully the difficult points addressed above, most notably the violent destruction of Israel's enemy Midian. The second is to root what is, at its heart, a description of a physical battle, in the New Covenant where battle lines have changed (see, for example Eph. 6:12).

What is clear from the passage is that its main theme is total victory in righteous battle. Even though the battle has some specific elements the overwhelming nature of the victory and the enormous battle spoils make it clear what is being conveyed.

Perhaps more than any other passage so far in the book of Numbers, great care should be given translating the lessons here into New Covenant equivalents. 'By the principles and standards set forth by Jesus Christ, the law of holy war has been superseded by the law of love. There is no successor to Israel as the theocratic kingdom in the Bible or in subsequent human history, no realm defined by ethnicity or national boundaries. The kingdom of God is still a theocracy, but it is defined by the Christian community of faith, those who have believed in Jesus as the Christ.'[4]

Getting the message clear: the aim

The passage needs to be seen in the light of the victory that Christ himself has won over our spiritual enemies

---

4   Cole, R.D., *The New American Commentary: Numbers* (Nashville, USA: Broadman & Holman, 2000), p. 492

(1 Cor. 15:57 [death], Col. 2:15 ['powers and authorities']). Our task is not so much to win the victory as to appropriate for ourselves what Christ has already won.

As such, this chapter of Numbers both illustrates the extent of Christ's victory and the way that Christians should fight to enjoy the benefits of the victory he has won.

A way in

Sandhurst cadets are taught *how* to fight. They learn tactics, manoeuvres, positions, weaponry and so on. All these are absent from this important chapter. It is not primarily about how to fight. Rather it shows how God's people celebrate the total victory that God wins. Christians need to know that it is Christ who has already won the victory for us. Our calling is to enjoy the battle outcome and this chapter of Numbers shows us how to do it.

Ideas for application

- The Christian journey is not an easy ride, but one where we need to face up to the realities of the dangers around us.

- Christian fighting needs to be ruthless; however we need to be clear about the exact enemies we are battling.

- Unlike the Israelites, Christians enjoy the battle already won for us by our Captain, the Lord Jesus.

- Enjoying the benefits of his victory should, if we have understood what he has done, lead to a spirit of overflowing thankfulness.

- Justice is absolute. Sin and rebellion must be punished to satisfy the justice of God.

Suggestions for preaching

When preaching or teaching this chapter we may need to establish some broad principles to address particular concerns that people may have about the apparent brutality of the fight. When preaching this chapter, I outlined three brief but important principles:

1. The annihilation was deserved. God's judgement is always just and right. Rather than blanche at the apparent barbarity of Numbers 31 we should be amazed at the justice of it. God is using the nation to be an instrument of his righteous anger.

2. Our battles are different. First, this is because the battles are spiritual not physical. In fact, we are to 'love your enemies and pray for those who persecute you' (Matt. 5:44). Second, this is because Christ has won the battles for us when he died on the cross.

3. Christians must battle with equal vigour. Though Christ has won our war, he still calls us to fight in the spiritual realms to appropriate the victory that he has secured.

Sermon 1

Numbers 31 shows us how to respond to the victory Christ has won (not, notice, how to win it ourselves).

+ **Be obedient** (vv. 1 and 7). Our refrain of obedience has returned! The people now do exactly what the Lord commands. The one who gives us victory says, 'Blessed rather are those who hear the word of God and obey it' (Luke 11:28). It's no accident that the alternative title for Numbers 'And the Lord said' drives this passage forward (vv. 1 and 25).

+ **Be focused** (v. 6). The Israelites carry the Ark into battle because it represents the very presence of God. As soon as we try to fight the battle ourselves rather than appropriating a victory Christ has already won for us, we shall be in trouble. Our fighting strategy is to look to the presence of the warrior King who is the Captain of our salvation.

+ **Be ruthless** (v. 15). It may feel inappropriate to draw lessons from the difficult passage at the heart of Numbers 31. However, the commands given to the people by Moses display a ruthlessness that will prevent sin from taking hold (see Num. 33:52). We need to have a similar view of sin which is to be 'put to death' amongst us (Rom. 8:13).

+ **Be thankful** (v. 25 onwards). The blessings of victory are extraordinarily abundant – no less, in the new covenant, than eternal life itself. The proper response is one of overflowing thankfulness.

Sermon 2

An alternative approach shifts the focus onto the character of God displayed through the chapter. For example, there are clear marks of justice, protection, provision and mercy (especially in the atonement of verse 50, depending on how it is understood).[5]

---

5   This is the approach taken by Brown, for example.

Suggestions for teaching

Questions to help understand the passage

1. What is the purpose behind this battle (see vv. 1-2)?

2. What are we told about the manner of the fighting (vv. 3-12)?

3. Why does this victory incur the wrath of Moses and Eleazar (vv. 15-16)?

4. This judgement seems very harsh to our 21st Century thinking. Why is it an appropriate sentence? (Check back with Numbers 25:1-3 for a reminder of the original sin).

5. What provision is made for those who have come into contact with dead bodies and why is it necessary (see vv. 19-24)?

6. How is the plunder divided (vv. 25-47)?

Questions to help apply the passage

1. How should we understand battle passages in the light of Jesus' work and his command to love our enemies? (Use 1 Cor. 15:57, Col. 2:15 and Eph. 6:12 for help).

2. How would you answer the objection that this passage shows that the God of the Old Testament is different from the God of the New?

3. What does this teach us about how Christians should battle and how we should enjoy the victory that Christ has won.

4. Read verses 48-54 again. How do the soldiers respond and what can we learn from their actions?

3
DISUNITY (32)

Introduction

We have already seen that the second census served an important secondary purpose – the division of the land by tribe and size. Now, in the otherwise positive second section of Numbers, we discover a moment that shows the new generation in a light that is less than positive. It is not a negative view of the entire generation, but of two particular tribes – Reuben and Gad (later joined by the half tribe of Manasseh – see v. 33).

Essentially two tribes decide that they would rather take land east of the Jordan than the promised land (which lays west of the Jordan). Chapter 32 outlines the request by the tribes and the steps taken by Moses to ensure that unity is maintained in the nation.

How one reads the text shapes how it might be preached or taught. Unusually, it is possible to see the passage teaching lessons that are quite opposite in nature. Some commentators, for example, see the lessons as broadly positive: "See how the two tribes help out their cousins! What a mark of unity!"[1] Others see the lessons as broadly negative: "See how the two tribes are not interested in the promised land! What a mark of disunity!"[2]

As we shall see below, I think the text encourages us to view the actions of the two tribes negatively: this makes the thrust of the passage about a rejection of God's word and promise, and the disunity that arises as a result. It still belongs in this second section because this is not a nationwide rebellion: the focus is very much on two tribes and their actions. We are not to assume anything negative about the majority of the nation who do not feature in this chapter at all.

Listening to the text

Context and structure

The victory battle against the Midianites has set the scene (at last!) for entry into the promised land. Though this entry will not be secured in the book of Numbers there is a last issue to resolve: two tribes prefer the land east of the Jordan. Chapter 32 works through the implications of this decision on their part and the steps that are taken to ensure the land west of the Jordan can still be taken in the same way the Midianites were defeated in chapter 31.

The structure is straightforward. Gad and Reuben make their request (vv. 1-5), Moses responds (vv. 6-15), the two

---

1   For example, 'It is possible to see in the actions of the men of Gad and Reuben nothing untoward at all, only a pragmatic decision that leads to a remarkable negotiation with the Lord and his servant Moses.' Allan, R. B. (1990), *Numbers.* In F. E. Gaebelein (Ed.), *The Expositor's Bible Commentary, Volume 2: Genesis, Exodus, Leviticus, Numbers* (Grand Rapids, USA: Zondervan, 1990), p. 975

2   For example, 'That any Israelite tribe should consider settling outside the land promised to Abraham showed a disturbing indifference to the divine word, the word on which Israel's existence entirely depended.' Wenham, p. 237

tribes make a counter-proposal (vv. 16-27) which Moses accepts. Then the final verses (28 to 42) show how the arrangement works out.

How should we view the request?
There are certainly signs that the request should be viewed positively. These include:

+ Although the request stokes Moses' anger (v. 14), there is no direct indication that God's anger is likewise aroused. We only have what Moses thinks the Lord *may* think.

+ Gad and Reuben are ready to put themselves on the line for the other tribes leaving women, children and flocks at home (v. 17). It could be argued that this is an act of faith rather than of disobedience.

+ Moses agrees to the second proposal of Gad and Reuben and seems to endorse their approach (v. 20). The land is then called a 'possession' (v. 22), a very significant technical term.

+ Verse 30 seems to suggest that the inheritance of land west of the Jordan is a privilege rather than a judgement.

+ The city renaming process in verses 34 to 42 seems to suggest that some pagan names are swapped for names which reflect Yahweh's own name (see below).

+ Joshua 22:2 records the moment when the tribes are released from their vow. It appears to look favourably upon what they have done: 'You have done all that Moses the servant of the Lord commanded, and you have obeyed me [Joshua] in everything I have commanded.'

However, the argument that their request is one of disobedience seems to fit more consistently with the thrust of the passage and the textual evidence:

+ The initial request asks for land outside the promised land. The two tribes are not unlike Lot who saw that the land was good (Gen. 13:10-13). The request demonstrates a rejection of the promise God has himself given regarding the land (see Num. 34:12).

+ The request ignores the God-given method for allocation of the land. It is not to be chosen by each tribe but given by God through lots (Num. 26:55). This is the way that the actual land is divided up in Numbers 34:13.

+ Moses' anger is not rebuked by Yahweh. There is no evidence in the text that Moses does not also reflect the views of the Almighty. Indeed, given his high status, this (unless there is evidence to the contrary) should be our default understanding of his reaction.

+ Moses uses the story of the rebellion of the spies (Num. 13–14) to rebuke the Reubenites and Gadites. Their disobedience seems to be of the same order – not wanting to cross the Jordan (v. 5).

+ The compromise suggested by the two tribes (see below for more detail) still has a ring of selfishness about it. The tribes are interested in what they can get. Nor does their lack of faith about the current inhabitants (see v. 17) fit with what chapter 31 has led us to expect. Moreover, their proposal rejects the marching order that God himself has given (compare v. 17 with 2:16).

+ The promise of land seems to have been turned into a curse (see v. 30). This strange *volte face* can only be explained by a negative view of the request and counter-proposal.

+ The numbers simply do not add up. According to Joshua 4:13 only 40,000 soldiers from the two tribes crossed the Jordan. This was out of a total of 84,280 (adding 26:7 and 26:18). That means that the positive words of Joshua 22 are only spoken to the faithful remnant who kept the promises made in Numbers 32.

+ Naming cities after Yahweh is no guarantee that Yahweh is being followed, honoured and obeyed.

+ Significantly, the first three tribes to be exiled were Reuben, Gad and Manasseh (1 Chron. 5:26).

These points, taken together, seem to point towards an unfavourable view of the actions of the two tribes.

Working through the text

The initial request (32:1-5)

The consistent biblical definition of Canaan is land west of the Jordan river (many Bibles contain a map of the tribal allocations). The Reubenites and Gadites ask for land outside of this boundary. It is good land for flocks and it is land that the Lord has previously subdued (see 21:21-31). However, as we shall soon learn, this does not mean that all the inhabitants have been removed (compare 31 with 32:17).

Their request, as noted above, contravenes the process the Lord himself has put in place to allocate the land (by lot and size). It is thus difficult not to read verse 5 in a negative light. Although the tribes will later offer military support for the Canaan campaign, it is initially absent. Given that the book of Numbers has emphasised the togetherness and equality of the nation (e.g. 31:4), the request marks the beginning of the break-up of the nation.

Moses' first response (32:6-15)

Moses responds with righteous anger, likening the request to the report given by the fearful spies in Numbers 13 (13:31-33). He accuses them of 'discouraging the Israelites' (v. 9), seeing their request as having a negative impact on the remaining tribes. Indeed, 'the Lord's anger was aroused that day' (v. 10) and all of the first generation were consigned to die in the wilderness. Must there be a repeat performance?

No wonder that Moses reserves strong language for them: 'a brood of sinners, standing in the place of your fathers [i.e. repeating their sin] and making the Lord even more angry with Israel' (v. 14). Their request could well be 'the cause of [Israel's] destruction' (v. 15).

There is no reason to suppose that Moses does not speak here for Yahweh himself. Certainly there are other times when he speaks rashly, but on each occasion that happens, his error is corrected. No such reversal occurs here.

The counter-proposal (32:16-19)

Hearing Moses' anger does not make the tribes withdraw their request, but they do significantly amend it. The amendment seeks to commit the troops to the battle if the women and children can stay behind (itself a risky approach – see v. 17). The rebellious tribes want to make clear that they understand they will not receive any inheritance in the land they are helping to clear because their 'inheritance' is east of the river.

Significantly, in his reply, Moses seems unable to use the same language. He does speak of the eastern land as a 'possession' (v. 29), but he baulks at the language of inheritance. It can hardly be that – it has been requested rather than granted.[3]

It may well be that the offer of troops in verse 17 is actually an offer of crack, elite soldiers – a kind of ancient SAS or SEAL unit.[4] If so, this makes sense of Moses second response which follows.

Moses' second response (32:20-27)

Moses makes it clear that he will countenance the counter proposal if 'all' the Reubenites and Gadites come to help (vv. 21, 27, 29). The repetition may well stand in contrast to the original offer of sending only the elite units. Whatever the meaning of verse 17, Joshua 4:13 demonstrates that the promise was not kept – only 40,000 out of 84,280 possible troops crossed into Canaan. Moreover, the troops will only be relieved of their obligation once the whole land is subdued (v. 22, compare Joshua 22:1-2).

Is this Moses accepting their proposal as good? Or rather, as most commentators see it, is it Moses accommodating plans to their sinful request? The tone seems to suggest the latter. Calvin sees it as 'God's indulgence, that which might justly have been injurious to them, turned out for their advantage.'[5]

Interestingly, Moses is clear that the actions of Reuben and Gad – even when amended by the counter-proposal – will put them out of fellowship with both the Lord and the nation: after that 'you may return and be free from your obligation to the

---

3   Although it should be noted that the inheritance language *is* used in 34:14.

4   This is the assessment of a Jewish commentator, Jacob Milgrom on what it means to be 'ready'.

5   Calvin, J., *Commentaries on the Four Last Books of Moses Arranged in the Form of a Harmony* (Bellingham, USA: Logos Bible Software, 2010) electronic edition.

Lord and to Israel' (v. 22). It may be that Moses is only referring to the specific obligation to help with fighting, but it is difficult not to sense a deeper divide that has been opened up.

Such is the importance of fighting together that Moses warns the two tribes that any failure to act according to their promise will be quickly discovered. In a phrase that has become proverbial (in the Authorised Version text) he tells them to be 'sure that your sin will find you out' (v. 23). 'Sin is a tireless pursuer when it comes to seek its just payment: like a shark that smells blood, it will never leave a wounded swimmer alone. It comes on relentlessly, seeking its wages, which are nothing less than eternal, spiritual death.'[6]

Practical arrangements (32:28-42)
Moses knows he will not be able to enter the promised land and so he passes on the agreement to Eleazar the priest (this is obviously a promise made before the Lord) and to Joshua. The repetition of the conditions (vv. 29-30) underline their binding nature – an agreement which the two tribes once again accept (vv. 31 and 32 parallel vv. 25 to 27). Only then is the territory allotted to them.[7]

Verses 34 to 38 identify cities included in the provision and whose names are changed. 'It was not appropriate for committed Israelite people to live in towns…dedicated to pagan deities. These people… acknowledged the Lord's goodness in giving them a new land.'[8] Perhaps, although changing the name of a city does not change the hearts of its inhabitants. It may simply be an outward gesture.

In the final verses we discover how it comes to be that some of the half tribe of Manasseh is grouped together with

---

6   Duguid, p. 343

7   Brown sees in the response repentance, trust and obedience but this seems to be reading too much into the text. Brown, pp. 286-7

8   Brown, p. 288

Reuben and Gad. It seems that one particular clan (Makir) had enjoyed some battle success in the region and wants to be treated as the Reubenites and Gadites. We are given no comment on this extraordinary development (Gilead is also outside of the promised land) other than Moses accedes to the request. It is clear that Moses' initial prediction (v. 7) is already coming true. The nation is no longer one.

From text to message

Getting the message clear: the theme
How the preacher or study leader understands the text shapes the theme. As explained above, I think it is best to see the text as a negative assessment of the action of the two tribes – actions which split the nation and contribute to Moses' initial assessment proved right in history – discouraging the other tribes. On this basis the theme is that the nation begins to fall apart after its initial united success.[9]

Getting the message clear: the aim
The Bible is clear about the danger of disunity. Christians are called to fight together because our Saviour, Christ Jesus, has drawn us together. He brings unity – we must 'make every effort to keep the unity of the Spirit through the bond of peace' (Eph. 4:3). The text paints a stark picture of how this disunity begins.

A way in
The very fact that it is not immediately clear whether the passage is describing a united nation or a disunited one provides a clear way in. Disunity is subtle, enticing –

---

9   John Currid sees the passage as teaching that we should keep our word – but surely this is the antithesis of what is being demonstrated? Reuben and Gad neither accept God's promises, nor – as the numbers show – keep their own promises. Currid, J, *Numbers* (Darlington, UK: Evangelical Press, 2009), p. 415

exciting even, but it always ends in tears. Any team sports illustration makes the point well – when individuals start playing for themselves and not for the team, the team rarely do well – even though there may be some exciting moments along the way.

The preacher or group leader will need to make it clear that the passage is best viewed as a negative commentary on the actions of Gad and Reuben. 'It is quite possible to pay lip service to the call of God, yet live at odds with it; to be under arms, it may be, and fighting the battles of the Lord, as Reuben was intending to do, but not with a full, unreserved commitment, and on a different footing from the real warriors of God.'[10]

Ideas for application

+ God calls his people to journey to the promised land together. Our propensity to disunity is destructive and puts our inheritance at risk.

+ Unity is centred on what God has done – here, on his rescuing and faithfulness in bringing his people to his inheritance. It is no surprise that Christian unity is centred on the Saviour.

+ Unity does not mean uniformity. Each tribe is different and will inherit different portions. Nevertheless, they are to battle and fight together.

Suggestions for preaching

Sermon 1

One approach is to take the theme of disunity and see how the text describes it. Such an approach will yield largely negative, but still valuable lessons.

---

10   Philip, p. 304

+ **Disunity begins with disobedience.** The tribes' request (vv. 1-5) is a rejection of God's promise. Moses is right to be spitting mad (vv. 6-15). Reading on in the story and seeing the tribes' offer of support, it is easy to forget that it begins with disobedience. Thankfully, God's grace and accommodation means that things do not turn out as badly as they might. But the nation is split by the rejection of God's good promises.

+ **Disunity can be dressed up as godliness.** It is interesting throughout that the tribes try to dress up their rebellion with godly language – for example, verse 4 or verse 31. In verses 34-38 they even change the names of their cities. This can make the beginnings of disunity hard to spot.

+ **Disunity can seem to be successful.** The other Israelites may have thought the offer of Gad and Reuben was win-win. They got to keep more land, yet still got the military help they needed to conquer Canaan. Sometimes, in the grace of God, disunity can seem to bring blessing. A church split can grow and see conversions. But that does not make the sin acceptable. [11]

The preacher will need to bring the lessons to a positive conclusion by showing that the source of our unity is Christ himself. He is our head and Captain and disunity should be impossible when we are fixed on him.

Sermon 2

Raymond Brown picks up on more of the detail of the passage in terms of the failure he sees in Gad and Reuben.[12] This may be an alternative approach, although he then sees

---

11   Not all divisions are wrong of course. Breaking with heterodoxy can sometimes be right.

12   Brown has some useful analysis at this point. Brown, p. 279

repentance and obedience in the latter part of the passage which may, I believe, be reading too much into the text. The lessons are still broadly negative.

Suggestions for teaching

Questions to help understand the passage

1. What do the two tribes request (vv. 1-5)?

2. Why is Moses so angry at what they ask (vv. 6-15)?

3. What should we think of the counter proposal of verses 16-19? Does it answer all of Moses' objections?

4. Why does Moses repeat the instructions he gives the tribes to Eleazar (see vv. 28-30)?

5. Do the Gadites and Reubenites keep their promises? Look up Joshua 4:13 and compare it with the Numbers 26 data. (You may like to ask, as an additional question, how this answer fits with Josh. 22:2.)

6. In broad terms, does the text make us think of these two tribes *positively* or *negatively*? Why?

Questions to help apply the passage

1. Where does Christian unity come from?

2. What has motivated the Gadites' and Reubenites' disunity? How may such things manifest themselves in churches today?

3. Do we share Moses' righteous anger at actions which promote disunity? Are we right to do so?

4. What effect on church life and mission does disunity have?

5. What can we do to 'make every effort to keep the unity of the Spirit through the bond of peace' (Eph. 4:3)?

4

ANTICIPATION (33–35)

Introduction

The story of Israel's wanderings in the desert is now drawing to a close and, as is appropriate for the tale of the second generation, the focus is now firmly on the promised land. At first glance, a section which is introduced with a backward looking review hardly seems to anticipate the conquest of Canaan. However, the God-ordained travelogue (33:2) doesn't just look backwards. It serves as a preparation for the final command to drive out the inhabitants of Canaan and take the land (33:50-56).

This segues neatly into a description of the promised land (ch. 34) and instructions for the setting up of cities of refuge (ch. 35). So, although these may seem disparate ideas, they are all joined together by the anticipation of the inheritance that awaits.

Listening to the text

Context and structure

The text divides neatly and obviously into four:

- A look back at the journey thus far (33:1-49)

- Instructions to take the land (33:50-56)

- Description of the boundaries of the land (34:1-29)

- Rules for the cities of refuge (35:1-34)

As with other sections in this story of the second generation, it is impossible to read through the passages without a sense of expectation: the Israelites are within touching distance of the promised land!

Working through the text

A look back at the journey (33:1-49)
It is easy to make *too* much of chapter 33. True, it is a record that is written down at the Lord's command (v. 2). This has led some commentators to see it as a kind of index to the book of Numbers, but there are several reasons why this is unlikely:

- The travelogue begins in Ramases (v. 5) and the first few stopover points (see table below) refer to incidents in the book of Exodus.

- Of the 40 place names, over half refer to places never mentioned in the book of Numbers. This makes its function as an index to the book highly dubious.

- The list does not reflect the balance of the book. All of the action subsequent to chapter 22 takes place on the plains of Moab which is hardly mentioned (vv. 48-49).

- Other places which feature in the Numbers account are omitted. These include Tabarah (11:3, which is important enough to feature in Moses' sermon in Deuteronomy 9:22) and Hormah (14:45). The whole travel section in 21:13-20 – significant enough to feature in the main text – is noticeable by its absence.

It is highly unlikely, therefore, that the list is meant to function as a guide to the book. Rather, it serves as a record of where the Israelites have journeyed and setting up the expectation of a final destination (which is the purpose of the following section).[1] 'The list of sites has the effect of levelling all the happenings of the last 40 years. [All the sites] are merely stopping places on the road to Canaan. And each stopping place… is a witness to the mighty grace of God who led the people on, in spite of all, toward the promised land.'[2]

The table below shows the complete list of names together with references to where the places occur in Numbers (or, in the first few cases, in Exodus). Most problematic for our purposes is the inclusion of Jotbathah (v. 33) which is also referenced in Deuteronomy 10:7 but as coming in a different place in the chronology. In the Deuteronomy passage, the site is listed after the death of Aaron whereas in this list it is included before his demise. It is not impossible, however, that the site was visited twice given the rather circuitous route that the wandering people took.

---

1   Wenham (p. 242) tabulates the list into six groups of seven seeing a pattern of cycles drawing attention to certain events in the nation's journey.

2   Ashley, p. 625

Ref.	Campsite	Reference	Notes
33:5	Ramases	Exodus 1:1	
33:5	Succoth	Exodus 12:37	
33:6	Etham	Exodus 13:20	
33:7	Pi Hahiroth (Migdol)	Exodus 14:2	Camped here to deceive Pharaoh
33:8	Marah	Exodus 15:23	First grumbling incident
33:9	Elim	Exodus 15:27	
33:10	Red Sea		
33:11	Desert of Sin	Exodus 16:1	Second grumbling incident
33:12	Dophkah	*	
33:13	Alush	*	
33:14	Rephidim	Exodus 17:1	Site of battle with Amalekites
33:15	Desert of Sinai	Numbers 1:1	
33:16	Kibroth Hattaavah	Numbers 11:35	Central grumbling section of Numbers
33:17	Hazeroth	Numbers 11:35	
33:18	Rithmah	*	
33:19	Rimmon Perez	*	
33:20	Libnah	*	
33:21	Rissah	*	
33:22	Kehelathah	*	
33:23	Mount Shepher	*	
33:24	Haradah	*	
33:25	Makheloth	*	
33:26	Tahath	*	
33:27	Terah	*	
33:28	Mithcah	*	
33:29	Hashmonah	*	
33:30	Moseroth	*	
33:31	Bene Jaakan	*	
33:32	Hor Haggidgad	*	
33:33	Jotbathah	*	Also in Deuteronomy 10:7 but in different chronology – perhaps visited twice?
33:34	Abronah	*	
33:35	Ezion Geber	*	Known elsewhere, e.g Deuteronomy 2:8

indicates that the site name does not appear elsewhere in the Numbers (or associated Exodus/Deuteronomy) account

A few places are considered worthy of expansion in the otherwise regular list of names:

+ Verse 3 describes in pithy summary the escape from Egypt after the tenth plague.

+ Verse 9 expands on the nature of Elim 'where there were twelve springs and seventy palm trees.' This is probably to contrast with the previous stopping place, Marah, which was the site of the infamous grumbling over water.

+ Mount Hor is recorded solemnly in verse 37 as the location of Aaron's death.

The list follows the same pattern throughout: 'They left... and camped at...' It ends with a final site using the same language, 'There on the plains of Moab they camped along the Jordan from Beth Jeshimoth to Abel Shittim' (v. 49). All the locations are thus temporary ones. This is not a description of permanence. That is anticipated.

Instructions to take the land (33:50-56)
The anticipation finds its fulfilment in the next short section. The word 'camp' disappears and is replaced by 'settle' (v. 53). Repeating some of the commands of earlier chapters (for example, 26:52-56), this passage reinforces the anticipatory nature of the travelogue.

There is both command and warning. The command to take the land and drive out the inhabitants comes in verses 50 to 54. In the light of the incidents at Abel Shittim (v. 49) the instruction is not simply to conquer the land but to rid it of its inhabitants and false gods. These are both wooden ('carved images', v. 52) and metal ('cast idols'). Israel is also to destroy the places associated with their worship ('the high places'[3]).

Failure to drive out the inhabitants will lead to future difficulties, not least because the current occupants will persist in their false religions. It's not just careless to let the Canaanites remain – it is deadly, 'then I will do to you what I plan to do to them' (v. 56). Given the story of Numbers so far, this warning should hardly be surprising. Judges 1 describes the sad failure of the tribes to heed these sober warnings.

Description of the boundaries of the land (34:1-29)

Chapter 34 now delineates the boundaries of the land. At no time in the Bible's recorded history did Israel ever inhabit this full territory.[4] The warnings of the previous verses prove to be true over the life of the nation. However, at this point in time, with the people faithful and eager to inherit, it is appropriate for Yahweh to lay out the maximum extent of the land to be given. It is clear, as is often the case when the land is discussed, that this is an inheritance that is *given* by God.

Many of the place names are obscure. Others are familiar but in strange locations – for example Mount Hor is here described as being in the north (34:7). There may be more than one such mountain. However, the overall point

---

3   A phrase which will become sadly common in the history of the kings of the nation.

4   For example, Israel only extended its borders to the Mediterranean in the second Century BC, an event described in the Eulogy of Simon in the apocryphal book of 1 Maccabees 14:5, 'to crown all his honours he took Joppa for a harbour and opened a way to the isles of the sea' (NRSV).

is crystal clear. The people are ready to inherit the promised land that the Lord will give. 'This will be your land' (v. 12). Notice that though there is grace in accepting the proposal of Gad, Reuben and Manasseh (vv. 13-15), their land is described as outside of the boundaries of the promised land.

Leaders are appointed to help divide the land – led by the two new men of the nation, Joshua and Eleazar (v. 16). This is now their time. Note that the list of names omits Gad and Reuben (further evidence that their land is outside the promised land that God gives).[5]

Rules for the cities of refuge (35:1-34)
A short paragraph now explains where the Levites are to reside. They have no inheritance because their task is to serve Yahweh (26:62). Where, however, are they to live? And what are they to do with their flocks given to them as spoil and tithe? The beginning of chapter 35 answers this question.

The number of cities to be given to the Levites is not specified until verse 7 (48 towns in total), but it is clear that provision is to be made for them to have somewhere to live. The key language of inheritance and possession is carefully avoided, but practical provision is still made.

Verses 4 and 5 seem, at first, to be contradictory. The pastureland of the cities shall extend 'fifteen hundred feet from the town wall.' However, the instruction is to measure 'three thousand feet' on each side. The problem is easily resolved, however, with a little maths! The side of the pastureland is the longer distance. If the pastureland approximates to a square, then each side is double the distance from the centre as shown in the diagram.

---

5   Manasseh is included because only part of this half tribe sought land outside the boundaries – see 32:39.

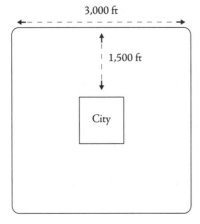

However, as the chapter progresses we discover that six of these cities are to serve a particular function. Life is not cheap to Yahweh, as he established in his covenant to Noah, 'Whoever sheds the blood of man, by man shall his blood be shed, for in the image of God has God made man' (Gen. 9:6). As the accounts of both Cain (Gen. 4:8) and Lamech (Gen. 4:23) have demonstrated from earliest times (and as the story of Moses has reinforced – see Exodus 2:12), murder is going to be an issue amongst a people so severely affected by sin.

Nevertheless, it is also possible for someone to be killed accidentally (what we might call manslaughter, though that term is not used in this passage). This section of Numbers makes provision for such a man or woman.

It does so by, first of all, establishing the six cities scattered throughout the land as places of refuge – three in the land of Gad and Reuben, three in the promised land. (One wonders why there seems to be an unequal division; are the two rebellious tribes more likely to kill? The explanation is more straightforward; the territory of Gad, Reuben and Manasseh is more diffuse than the concentrated promised land). These cities are to be 'a place of refuge...so that anyone who has killed another accidentally can flee there' (v. 15). How, though, are these cities to operate so that justice is done?

The next two paragraphs explain the operation. A murderer – someone who uses a weapon (an iron object, a stone or a club) shall not be able to use the cities. He shall be put to death. The 'avenger of death' – a technical term describing the nearest relative who deserves retribution – will be the one to enact the sentence. Similarly someone who kills another with 'malice aforethought' (which sounds like legal jargon, the ESV translates this phrase better as 'out of hatred') shall be put to death.

However, where someone is killed 'without hostility' (v. 22) and there was no intent, then the 'assembly must judge between him and the avenger of blood according to these regulations' (v. 24). Presumably the regulations are the questions asked by the previous passage – i.e. was the accused carrying a weapon and was there hostile intent. If there has been no murder then the accused must return to the city of refuge (to which he first fled) where he must live until the death of the high priest (v. 25). Like the Year of Jubilee, the death of the high priest marks a regular passing of an era.

However, should he ever leave the city of refuge (vv. 26-28) and he is discovered by the avenger, the avenger is at liberty to seek retribution for the death of his relative. Killing someone, on this basis, is not cheap. Even the man or woman found guilty of the lesser crime of manslaughter must pay a price of restricted freedom.

The final verses provide some additional rulings, often repeating what is stated elsewhere:

+ A murderer cannot be put to death on the testimony of only one witness (v. 30, compare Deut. 17:6).

+ A murderer cannot pay a ransom for his crime – his blood is required (v. 31).

+ Likewise, someone guilty of manslaughter cannot buy his way out of his enforced sentence (v. 32).

These rather sobering requirements and reminders that sin is ugly and present are necessary because 'bloodshed pollutes the land' and the only atonement for bloodshed is shed blood (v. 33). Just as Yahweh dwelt in the camp (5:3) so he will dwell in the land he is giving (v. 34).

From text to message

Getting the message clear: the theme
This group of chapters is the final piece of the jigsaw that is required to make it possible to enter into the promised land. Here the boundaries of the land are set and rules for living in the land established. The Israelites are nearly there.

Getting the message clear: the aim
These chapters reinforce key truths which are not new to Numbers but come at an important moment in the nation's history. Here are lessons they must learn if they are to inherit. Here are lessons for Christians that are essential to journeying successfully with Christ Jesus.

A way in
Everyone who has ever travelled with children knows the refrain, 'Are we nearly there yet?' Most of the time the answer is, sadly, 'No, not yet. Still an hour to go.' How refreshing it is to be able to say to the kids, 'Yes, this time we are nearly there.' And it's that moment when the front seat occupants tell the back seat children to get ready; make sure shoes are on, clothes straight, wide awake ready for the arrival. Here

then are some last instructions because the Israelites are nearly there.

Ideas for application

+ Backwards reflection is useful for future faithfulness. Journeying towards a certain destination requires some thinking about where we have come from.

+ There will still be sin in Israel's promised land; in contrast, though our journey to the promised land is plagued by sin, our inheritance is delightfully free from sin and its effects.

+ The taking of life, in particular, is a significant problem because human life is precious to Yahweh. This fact magnifies the cost that Christ paid to atone for all sins.

Suggestions for preaching

These three chapters constitute a large section which could be taken separately, although a series on Numbers could be very long if such an approach were taken. Whether this would be a wise course of action or not would depend largely on the nature of the congregation – what they were used to and what the preacher or Bible group leader felt they could handle. In some of the more detailed commentaries (e.g. Duguid) there are some useful pointers to preaching through this set of chapters more slowly.

However, if the chapters are to be taken together, a suggested approach is shown below.

Sermon 1

This approach tries to draw out the lessons from each of the three chapters.

- ✦ **Remember the past but focus on the future** (ch. 33). This chapter is clearly constructed to provide a way to remember what has happened in the past (and not just good things but the sinful moments too). However, it ends with a forward focus which contains both encouragement about the future alongside warning about losing ruthlessness when it comes to Yahweh's enemies.

- ✦ **Remember the prize is given by the Lord** (ch. 34). There is a very strong emphasis on the fact that the land is an inheritance, given by Yahweh to his people. As they undertake the very real task of battling for the land, they must never think that it is either theirs by right, nor that its conquest is their own achievement. This description of the promised land – large almost beyond belief – is proof positive that it is the Lord's doing.

- ✦ **Remember the pain that there will be along the way** (ch. 35). This strange chapter (in terms of its inclusion here) serves as a reminder that the people are not sinless and there will be trouble along the way. God graciously accommodates the provision to allow for the sin that is inherent in the people and so the chapter injects a dose of realism into the people. Yes, they are to look to Yahweh and battle for the promised land that he gives. But they must expect that the path will be narrow with many obstacles along the way.

The preacher or Bible study leader will have to root each of these points in our identity in Christ Jesus remembering that Christ the rock was with the Israelites as they journeyed.

Suggestions for teaching

Questions to help understand the passage

1. Review the place names in 33:1-49. Why do some warrant extra explanation do you think (e.g. vv. 3-4, v. 37)?

2. What is the link between this backward look and the material which immediately follows it (vv. 50-54)?

3. What sober warning accompanies the passage (vv. 55-56)? Why is this needed?

4. Read through chapter 34. Who is the hero of this passage, i.e. who gives the land? Why will the Israelites need to remember this?

5. The arrangements of chapter 35 seem a little bleak. Why are such realistic measures necessary as the people of God prepare to enter the promised land?

Questions to help apply the passage

1. What is the value of looking back? How does this sit with what Paul says in Philippians 3:13-14?

2. What will happen if Christians display a lack of ruthlessness when it comes to dealing with sin (see 33:55-56)?

3. As we journey towards our promised land, why do we need to remember that it is the Lord who gives us our inheritance? What sins might we fall into if we forget this important truth?

Chapter 35 arises from a realistic view of the effect of indwelling sin, even after the land has been conquered.

4. How can Christians reconcile this with the truth that God, by his Spirit, is transforming us into the likeness of Christ?

5. Why is this realistic view of life important in church life?

5

Inheritance (27 & 36)

Introduction

It seems fitting to end the story of Numbers, and the story of the second generation (for this book, at least) with the account of five heroines of the faith – their names are recorded three times for posterity (in Num. 26:33, 27:1 and 36:11). The repetition is no accident; these are names worth knowing for their actions display that they understand the importance of the land and are faithful and keen to possess it.

It is easy to be side-tracked in their story into issues of women's rights: are the two accounts a kind of early emancipation movement or, on the other hand, do they both demonstrate the kind of misogyny we might expect from this period of history? For the record, they tend to elevate the position of women in the culture of the day. However, that is hardly the point, and the preacher or group leader must not spend too much time in that particular "by-path meadow."

Listening to the text

Context and structure

The story takes place in two instalments or scenes. Scene I takes place immediately after the census where the issue is raised of whether the five daughters can inherit land (27:1-11). Scene II takes place in chapter 36. Here the issue is how the land the daughters have inherited can be kept in the ancestral tribe when marriage takes place. The second time around the issue is initiated by the tribal leaders – but the daughters still take centre stage as they assent to the new ruling (36:10-12).

Working through the text

Scene I: Daughters inheriting the land (27:1-11)

The daughters of Zelophehad are introduced right at the start of Scene I, though this is not the first time we have met them. They are mentioned in the census count of chapter 26 – either because the text anticipates the issue that will be raised in chapter 27 or, more likely, because they are the only family in this particular predicament.

The national and spiritual importance of their request is made clear in verse 2. They present themselves to 'the Tent of Meeting and stood before Moses, Eleazar the priest, the leaders and the whole assembly.' The issue is straightforward. Their father, Zelophehad died in the wilderness (as did all the parents of their generation). He had five daughters, but no sons. Importantly, he was not one of the Korah rebels (belonging to that rebellion would have forfeited all rights to an inheritance).

'Why should our father's name disappear from his clan because he had no son? Give us property among our father's relatives' (v. 4). In other words, please include us in the count of chapter 26 which is used to divide up the land.

Such a request sounds a little presumptuous – especially as it is presented in English translations ('give to us...'[1]). However, Yahweh's response shows us we are to think positively about their request: 'What Zelophehad's daughters are saying is right. You must certainly give them property as an inheritance among their father's relatives and turn their father's inheritance over to them' (v. 6)

This new case law is important. We know that because Moses has to seek counsel from the Lord himself – this is not a situation he can unilaterally decide upon (c.f. the situation in chapter 32). Moreover, the ruling needs clarification. It is not just to be an accommodation to these particular five women – but extended for all Israel's life.

In verses 8-11 a 'legal requirement' is established for all of Israel – land must be preserved in the family if at all possible and will pass through son, then through daughter if there is no son. If there is no offspring, the land will go to a brother, thereafter to uncles, thereafter to the 'nearest relative.' The current prescription was not meant to replace the normal line of descent through the male heirs, but to make an appropriate exemption when the conditions warranted.'[2]

It is easy to think that the five daughters are bit-part players in the scene that unfolds. However, we should remember that the request comes at their instigation. They understand that the great prize to be laid hold of by faith is the land that God has promised. They are faithful because they want to be part of that inheritance.

---

1   The verb could equally be translated 'grant to us...' which might seem less aggressive.

2   Ashley, p. 546

Scene II: Restricted marriage to keep the land in the tribe (36:1-13)

Now the issue is settled, we might think we have heard the last of Mahlah, Tirzah, Hoglah, Milcah and Noah.[3] After all, this generation is the one that will inherit the land and now provision has been made for families without male offspring.

However, there is a possible complication which arises and is resolved in chapter 36. Moses receives a new delegation from the women's clan. This particular clan is Gilead, descended through Makir from Manasseh. We have since learnt that this sub-clan has asked for land outside of the promised land (see 32:39). Interestingly, no comment is made (positive or negative) about that request – probably because the case law needs to be settled for the entire nation.

The new situation arises because the five daughters of Zelophehad may marry outside of their tribe. 'When the year of Jubilee comes, their inheritance will be added to that of the tribe into which they marry, and their property will be taken from the tribal inheritance of our forefathers' (v. 4).

This is an issue for the future. It is perhaps now, more than any other moment in Numbers, that we feel the certainty of the inheritance for now we are trying to resolve issues that will take place well into the future. The Year of Jubilee legislation – a kind of catch-all ruling which took place every fifty years – returned land and people to their own tribes (see Lev. 25:10). Clearly the understanding here is that it would mean a permanent move of land from one tribe to another.

---

3   The order of names is changed between chapters 26/27 and 36. We cannot say exactly why. It may reflect marital status.

Such a change is geographically problematic. Imagine a situation where pockets of land in one tribes' allotment belong to other tribes. The integrity of a tribe's God-given allocation is at risk.

However, the issue is not simply geographic. It is also spiritual. The inheritance of the promised land is of extraordinary significance. Land cannot be traded or given away with no thought for the consequences (as the story of Naboth's vineyard ably demonstrates – see 1 Kings 21).

Once again, this requires a ruling from Yahweh himself. And once again, he commends the original query, 'what the tribe of the descendants of Joseph is saying is right' (v. 5). The ruling is simple – inheriting daughters, like the daughters of Zelophehad – may not marry outside of their own tribal clan (v. 8). This will have the effect of ensuring that 'no inheritance may pass from tribe to tribe' (v. 9).

In the second part of the story we are told how the daughters of Zelophehad react. Remember this is a more restrictive ruling than chapter 27. However, the by-now-familiar refrain is applied unreservedly to the five women. 'So Zelophehad's daughters did as the Lord commanded Moses. Zelophehad's daughters – Mahlah, Tirzah, Hoglah, Milcah and Noah – married their cousins on their father's side. They married within the clans of the descendants of Manasseh, son of Joseph, and their inheritance remained in their father's clan and tribe' (vv. 11-12).

It may, at first, seem like this is a rather damp ending to a book which has been full of adventure and action. But nothing could be further from the truth. The journey has all been about getting to the promised land. Now we have five daughters who not only understand that the land is the main thing, but are willing to do whatever it takes to keep the inheritance within their family.

It might be argued that with 52,700 men from Manasseh to choose from, the ruling is hardly limiting their choices. However, as any parent knows, limiting marriage options is hardly likely to be a guarantee of success.

We are meant, therefore, to read this last chapter full of admiration for the five heroines. 'And note that this case so carefully recorded appears trivial, and unworthy of the space it occupies in Holy Writ. Nevertheless, it was not trivial, because it involved a most important principle, and because it was settled by an act of perfect obedience.' [4]

However, though the story's focus is on the five women, the text also makes clear throughout that it is the Lord who gives the land and needs to be consulted on how it can be preserved. The two passages are full of covenant land language ('possession' and 'inheritance') and the manner in which the Lord's counsel is sought highlights that any inheritance is only ever a gracious provision from a merciful and kind God.

From text to message

Getting the message clear: the theme
Yahweh both grants and preserves the inheritance he gives his people. This theme lifts the focus appropriately away from the five daughters. Their requests and willingness to go along with whatever the Lord decides is their obedient response to what he is doing.

Getting the message clear: the aim
Christians need to understand that God who gives us our inheritance also preserves it for us (see, for example,

---

4   H.D.M. Spence-Jones, *The Pulpit Commentary, Numbers* (London, UK: Funk & Wagnalls, 1910), p. 460

1 Pet. 1:3-5). Our appropriate response is to find security in him and to do all that he commands.

A way in

If someone gives you something very valuable you are going to take whatever steps are needed to preserve it. Up to now, the entire focus of the book of Numbers has been on reaching the promised land. But what if, right on the brink of entry, there is a risk that the land might be snatched away from a family because there are no male heirs to inherit?

We need to realise that property which passes down a male line seems an increasingly obscure idea. Indeed, at the time of writing, the UK Government is changing the law so that female heirs of the King or Queen will take their rightful place in the line of succession. However, the preacher or leader has to attempt to introduce the chapters not by an appeal to fair treatment of men and women (that is not the issue here) but, rather, to how the precious thing that God gives (the land) may be preserved and enjoyed.

Ideas for application

+ The two passages stress the God-given nature of inheritance. Ultimately it is this fact which makes inheritance secure.

+ Once given, the Lord also rules to ensure that the inheritance is rightly preserved.

+ The land (or 'rest') is a key idea throughout Scripture and finds its fulfilment in our own promised land, our eternal salvation or rest in Christ Jesus. This is the end goal of our salvation.

♦   The passages thus give Christians an eternal focus to
    life which they often lack.

♦   The appropriate response to God's giving and
    preservation is to do as the Lord commands. True
    faith always leads to obedience and eternal focus has
    an impact on how we live now.

Suggestions for preaching

These two sections, though several chapters apart, fit naturally
together in a series that deals with Numbers at the pace at
which we have been travelling. There are the same characters,
the same issue (preservation of land) and the same outcome
(the Lord's agreement and the women's obedience). The two
problems (inheritance in chapter 27 and preservation in
chapter 36) are issues of being in the promised land. This is
thus an appropriate finish to the book.

The preacher or teacher needs to work hard to avoid
too much time spent on issues of equality or emancipation.
Those are not the primary concern of the text.

Sermon 1

The best kind of sermon focuses on what the two passages
teach us about the Lord, illustrated from the situation of
the five women.

♦   **Faithful servants[5] know that it is the Lord who gives
    the inheritance** (ch. 27). It is clear that God gives the
    land. That is why this particular difficult situation must
    be brought to Moses who seeks the Lord's counsel.

---

5   On women's conferences and in women's groups I have preached
this sermon as 'Faithful *women…*' rather than *servants*. However, in a mixed
congregation, the preacher needs to ensure that his sermon headings include all
listeners, both men and women.

This difficulty cannot be resolved any other way. As an ending to the book of Numbers it is appropriate to remind ourselves that we cannot ever claim that anyone has earned their own portion of the land. The daughters of Zelophehad see this and demonstrate faith by laying hold of what their parents' generation threw away so casually. The passage encourages us therefore to have a proper focus on what really counts in eternity and what God gives to us in Christ.

* **Faithful servants know that it is the Lord who preserves the inheritance** (ch. 36). Having received their inheritance by faith there is a real risk that events may transpire to have it removed from them. The tribal leaders (along with the five women) recognise this and approach the Lord to ensure that the land stays in the tribe. The people have no suggestion to make to Yahweh: he himself provides the solution (v. 5). Though the women must respond in obedience to the Lord's command (v. 10), it is ultimately the Lord who intervenes to ensure that the inheritance is kept, even when it means going against the culture and practice of the day.

Alternative approaches

Most commentaries or books of sermons that progress through Numbers at a slower pace would take chapters 27 and 36 separately, as befits their position in the text. If this approach is taken, then the focus in the first story clearly needs to be on the way that the inheritance God gives is appropriated by faith. The focus on the second story is the preservation of the inheritance God gives, again appropriated by faith.

Suggestions for teaching

Questions to help understand the passage

1. What is the issue raised in 27:1-11?

2. Why does Moses bring their case before the Lord (27:5) rather than ruling on it himself?

3. How does the Lord answer?

4. What is the follow up issue raised in 36:1-4?

5. How does the Lord answer this time?

6. How do the five daughters of Zelophehad respond to this requirement (see 36:10-12)?

Questions to help apply the passage

1. What is the inheritance that Christians (and these women) ultimately look to? Look up Hebrews 11:13-16 for help.

2. Where does this inheritance come from? (See 1 Pet. 1:3)

3. Is our inheritance safe? How so? (See 1 Pet. 1:4-5)

4. How does the response of the daughters help us see how we should respond to God's gracious work?

5. What other things might we be tempted to make the 'main thing' rather than the eternal inheritance God gives us in Christ Jesus? How can we keep our eyes fixed on the prize?

EPILOGUE

The book of Numbers comes to an apparently abrupt end. However, it is entirely appropriate that we end the story with a focus on five people (women, as it happens) who understand the precious nature of the inheritance that God gives and who walk by faith as they look forward. 'All these people were still living by faith when they died. They did not receive the things promised; they only saw them from a distance. And they admitted that they were aliens and strangers on earth. People who say such things show that they are looking for a country of their own...they were looking for a better country – a heavenly one. Therefore God is not ashamed to be their God, for he has prepared a city for them' (Heb. 11:13-16).

FURTHER READING

There are a number of excellent commentaries on Numbers. They mainly fall into two categories. There are those which I call *devotional*. These are largely based on sermons and will tend to be good help for application and structure. However, as with any such resource, there is always a temptation simply to preach the sermons of someone else. I tend to use these sparingly in sermon preparation; however they are, by definition, the most accessible. Duguid's is the best volume for a preacher. If a congregation member wants a useful help then Pakula's is best or the *Introducing Numbers* volume that accompanies this series.

+ Raymond Brown, *Bible Speaks Today, Numbers* (Nottingham, UK: IVP, 2002)

+ Iain Duguid, *Numbers: God's presence in the wilderness* (Wheaton, USA: Crossway, 2006)

+ Martin Pakula, *Homeward Bound: reading Numbers today* (Sydney, Australia: Aquila Press, 2006)

- James Philip, *The Preacher's Commentary Volume 4* (Nashville, USA: Thomas Nelson, 1987)

Analytical commentaries tend to consider the text on a verse by verse basis. I find these most useful for getting to the bottom of particular difficult issues or providing insights into the Hebrew text that scholars can sometimes bring. These more technical commentaries often discuss at great length the originality of the text and other issues with which the evangelical preacher need not wrestle too much! I found Ashley's volume most help, though Wenham's Tyndale contribution is superbly thorough for a small book.

- Timothy Ashley, *NICOT Numbers* (Grand Rapids, USA: Eerdmans, 1993)

- Richard Boyce, *Leviticus and Numbers* (Louisville, USA: Wesminster John Knox Press, 2008)

- Dennis Cole, *The New American Commentary Volume 3b* (Nashville, USA: Broadman & Holman, 2000)

- Philip Budd, *Word Biblical Commentary Volume 5* (Dallas, USA: Word, 1984)

- Dennis Olson, *Numbers* (Louisville, USA: Westminster John Knox Press, 1996)

- Gordon Wenham, *Numbers: an introduction and commentary* (Nottingham, UK: IVP, 1981)

Also excellent are the study notes written by Wenham in ed. Dennis T. Lane, ESV *Study Bible* (Wheaton, USA: Crossway Books, 2008).

PT RESOURCES

RESOURCES FOR PREACHERS AND BIBLE TEACHERS

PT Resources, a ministry of The Proclamation Trust, provides a range of multimedia resources for preachers and Bible teachers.

Teach the Bible Series (Christian Focus & PT Resources)
The Teaching the Bible Series, published jointly with *Christian Focus Publications*, is written by preachers, for preachers, and is specifically geared to the purpose of God's Word – its proclamation as living truth. Books in the series aim to help the reader move beyond simply understanding a text to communicating and applying it.

Current titles include: *Teaching 1 Peter, Teaching 1 Timothy, Teaching Acts, Teaching Amos, Teaching Ephesians, Teaching Isaiah, Teaching John, Teaching Matthew, Teaching Numbers, Teaching Romans, Teaching the Christian Hope* and *Spirit of Truth*

Forthcoming titles include: *Teaching Daniel, Teaching 1 and 2 Kings,* and *Teaching Nehemiah.*

Practical Preacher series

PT Resources publish a number of books addressing practical issues for preachers. These include *The Priority of Preaching*, *Bible Delight* and *Hearing the Spirit*. Forthcoming titles include *The Ministry Medical* (ISBN 978-1-78191-232-4), a ministry checklist based on the book of 2 Timothy.

Online resources

We publish a large number of audio resources online, all of which are free to download. These are searchable through our website by speaker, date, topic and Bible book. The resources include:

+ sermon series; examples of great preaching which not only demonstrate faithful principles but which will refresh and encourage the heart of the preacher

+ instructions; audio which helps the teacher or preacher understand, open up and teach individual books of the Bible by getting to grips with their central message and purpose

+ conference recordings; audio from all our conferences including the annual Evangelical Ministry Assembly. These talks discuss ministry and preaching issues.

An increasing number of resources are also available in video download form.

Online DVD

PT Resources have recently published online our collection of instructional videos by David Jackman. This material has been taught over the past 20 years on our PT Cornhill training course and around the world. it gives step by step instructions on handling each genre of biblical literature.

There is also an online workbook. The videos are suitable for preachers and those teaching the Bible in a variety of different contexts. Access to all the videos is free of charge.

The Proclaimer

Visit the Proclaimer blog for regular updates on matters to do with preaching. This is a short, punchy blog refreshed daily which is written by preachers and for preachers. It can be accessed via the PT website or through www.theproclaimer.org.uk.

'Teaching' titles from
Christian Focus and PT Resources

Teaching Numbers
ISBN 978-1-78191-156-3

Teaching Isaiah
ISBN 978-1-84550-565-3

Teaching Daniel
ISBN 978-1-84550-457-1
(Summer 2014)

Teaching Amos
ISBN 978-1-84550-142-6

Teaching Matthew
ISBN 978-1-84550-480-9

Teaching John
ISBN 978-1-85792-790-0

Teaching Acts
ISBN 978-1-84550-255-3

**Teaching Romans
(volume 1)**
ISBN 978-1-84550-455-7

**Teaching Romans
(volume 2)**
ISBN 978-1-84550-456-4

Teaching Ephesians
ISBN 978-1-84550-684-1

Teaching 1 Timothy
ISBN 978-1-84550-808-1

Teaching 1 Peter
ISBN 978-1-84550-347-5

Teaching the Christian Hope
ISBN 978-1-85792-518-0

Spirit of Truth
ISBN 978-1-84550-057-3

About the Proclamation Trust

We exist to promote church-based expository Bible ministry and especially to equip and encourage Biblical expository preachers because we recognise the primary role of preaching in God's sovereign purposes in the world through the local church.

Biblical (the message)
We believe the Bible is God's written Word and that, by the work of the Holy Spirit, as it is faithfully preached God's voice is truly heard.

Expository (the method)
Central to the preacher's task is correctly handling the Bible, seeking to discern the mind of the Spirit in the passage being expounded through prayerful study of the text in the light of its context in the biblical book and the Bible as a whole. This divine message must then be preached in dependence on the Holy Spirit to the minds, hearts and wills of the contemporary hearers.

Preachers (the messengers)
The public proclamation of God's Word by suitably gifted leaders is fundamental to a ministry that honours God, builds the church and reaches the world. God uses weak jars of clay in this task who need encouragement to persevere in their biblical convictions, ministry of God's Word and godly walk with Christ.

We achieve this through:

+ PT Cornhill: a one year full-time or two-year part-time church based training course

+ PT Conferences: offering practical encouragement for Bible preachers, teachers and ministers' wives

+ PT Resources: including books, online resources, the PT blog (www.theproclaimer.org.uk) and podcasts

Christian Focus Publications

Our mission statement –

STAYING FAITHFUL

In dependence upon God we seek to impact the world through literature faithful to His infallible Word, the Bible. Our aim is to ensure that the Lord Jesus Christ is presented as the only hope to obtain forgiveness of sin, live a useful life and look forward to heaven with Him.

Our books are published in four imprints:

CHRISTIAN
FOCUS

Popular works including biographies, commentaries, basic doctrine and Christian living.

CHRISTIAN
HERITAGE

Books representing some of the best material from the rich heritage of the church.

MENTOR

Books written at a level suitable for Bible College and seminary students, pastors, and other serious readers. The imprint includes commentaries, doctrinal studies, examination of current issues and church history.

CF4•K

Children's books for quality Bible teaching and for all age groups: Sunday school curriculum, puzzle and activity books; personal and family devotional titles, biographies and inspirational stories – because you are never too young to know Jesus!

Christian Focus Publications Ltd,
Geanies House, Fearn, Ross-shire,
IV20 1TW, Scotland, United Kingdom.
www.christianfocus.com